Shiloh

Hell, on Earth

Line of Battle Book 2

Copyright © 2019 Nick Vulich

Table of Contents

Introduction 1
Civil War Timeline—1862..4
Participants 39
Pittsburg Landing, or the Battle of Shiloh 56
Cincinnati Gazette Account...75
Account of James R. Scott...133
Account of Sgt. H. M. White..136
Cincinnati Times Account..148
Footnotes 154

Introduction

The Battle of Pittsburg Landing or Shiloh was a major Union victory, but General Ulysses S. Grant had reservations.

Newspapers attacked Grant and Sherman for not digging entrenchments and throwing out more pickets to prevent being taken by surprise. General Don Carlos Buell accused him of being unorganized and incompetent by letting his men be taken entirely by surprise on the morning of April 6th. Regular soldiers were just as frustrated. Sergeant H. M. White wrote a friend about the change in atmosphere once General Don Carlos Buell arrived: "Today we had generalship, yesterday chance seemed to rule the hour. The change was miraculous. For the first time we could perceive the difference between a scientific soldier, for such Buell assuredly is, and an imbecile character [General Grant], which term describes somebody else."[1]

More perplexing for Grant was the way his superior, General Henry Halleck treated him after the battle. When Halleck rode into Pittsburg Landing a few days after the battle ended, he didn't have any kind words for Grant.

Grant never forgot the way Halleck treated him. "General Halleck moved his troops to Pittsburg Landing and assumed command of the troops in the field," wrote

Grant. "Although next to him in rank, and nominally in command of my old district and army, I was ignored... I was not permitted to see one of the reports of General Buell or his subordinates in that battle."[2]

Before the end of the month, Halleck reorganized his army into three separate wings: General George H. Thomas, had command of the right wing; General Don Carlos Buell took command of the center wing; and John Pope commanded the left wing. John McClernand held the reserve.

Halleck named Grant his second in command. Similar, to vice president, he had a lofty position, but no power. General Sherman observed that "Grant was substantially left out... with no clear, well defined command or authority." He took it as well as he could, but Sherman "could see that he felt deeply the indignity, if not insult, heaped upon him."[3]

It was a strange way to treat the commander of an army who had just won a major victory.

By May, Grant was so confused about the situation he had requested a thirty-day furlough to think things over. Sherman understood, but put in his two-cents worth: "Before the battle of Shiloh," he told Grant, "I had been cast down by a newspaper assertion of 'crazy;' but that single battle had given me new life, and now I was in high feather; and I argued with him, if he went away, events would go right along, and he would be left out; whereas, if he remained, some happy accident might restore him to favor and his true place."[4]

And, sure enough, it happened.

Beauregard abandoned Corinth on May 30th. Halleck's army marched in and took control of the city without firing a shot. Secretary of War Edwin Stanton called it a "brilliant and successful achievement." Halleck believed them, thinking his strategy brought about the great victory.

Lincoln and Stanton placed Halleck in command of the entire army in early July. As soon as Halleck rode off to Washington Grant resumed command of the Army of Tennessee.

Civil War Timeline—1862

January 8.

General Ambrose Burnside's army of 13,000 men sets sail from Annapolis, Maryland to Stumpy Point, North Carolina, preparatory to their attack on Roanoke Island. After facing storms and other mishaps at sea, they arrive off the coast of Roanoke Island nearly a month later, on February 6th.

January 19.

The Battle of Mill Springs (Kentucky) is the first major Union victory of the war. Confederate General Felix K. Zollicoffer dies in the fighting when he accidentally wanders into Union lines.

February 6.

General Ulysses S. Grant plans a coordinated attack on Fort Henry with the Union Navy. Bad weather swamps the roads and slows his march. By the time he arrives at Fort Henry, the Navy, under Flag Officer Andrew Hull Foote has taken the fortress. After the battle, General Lloyd Tilghman, the commander of the Fort Henry, says the site selected for the fort did not have one "redeeming feature" to enable him to defend it.

Grant informs General Halleck he will take Fort Donelson on February 8th. He might have done it, except the rain won't let up. It mucks up the roads and grinds his advance to a halt.

February 7

General Ambrose Burnside launches his attack on Roanoke Island (North Carolina) about 11:30 am. Union artillery bombards Fort Bartow and the small Confederate "Mosquito Fleet" destroying two boats—the Curlew and Forrest. That night, as Fort Bartow burns from the Union bombardment, Burnside lands his entire force on shore.

February 8.

Burnside's troops march on Fort Bartow. When they get there, they discover the three-gun battery is protected by a water-filled ditch three foot deep. After fierce fighting, the Confederates abandon their guns and run back to their camps. Burnside captures 2500 prisoners with a loss of just 37 killed, and 214 wounded.

February 10.

The Federal Navy battles the Confederate "Mosquito Fleet," this time on the Pasquotank River near Elizabeth City (North Carolina). After the Battle of Roanoke, Flag Officer William Lynch takes what remains of his fleet to Elizabeth City. The Union fleet arrives on February 10th. In less than an hour, they destroy the Confederate fleet and silence the guns at nearby Cobbs Point.

February 12

Grant's troops arrive outside of Fort Donelson (Tennessee). He is overconfident and cocky going into the battle because he believes General Pillow is overcautious and would not send his troops out of his fortifications to attack him. He is wrong.

February 13.

Federal troops and gunboats open a concentrated fire on Fort Donelson early in the morning. Grant's infantry makes a series of charges that day but experiences little success.

February 14.

Flag Officer Foote's gunboats attack Fort Donelson but are forced to retire after crushing fire from the fort's batteries. Grant's men continue slugging away at the fort.

February 15.

The rebels leave their rifle pits and make a mad dash for the Federal forces. Fierce fighting takes place over the next seven hours. Finally, Grant orders General Charles. F. Smith to storm one of the redoubts. The regiment "which was raked by musketry, grape, and canister, without firing a gun; swept over the breastworks, drove the rebels from their hiding places, and planted their flags on the rebel fortifications."[5]

February 16.

Union forces are taken by surprise early in the morning when the rebels hoist a white flag of surrender. Thirteen thousand troops are taken prisoner. Several thousand more escape during the night with Generals John Floyd and Gideon Johnson Pillow. Another thousand cavalry troopers make their exit with Nathan Bedford Forrest.

Nearly 1,000 soldiers lay dead on the field. The men that bullet and shot miss, the cold takes care of.

General Grant earns the name "Unconditional Surrender" when he tells his old friend General Simon Bolivar Buckner: "No terms except unconditional and immediate surrender can be accepted. I propose to move immediately upon your works."[6]

February 23.

After the fall of Forts, Henry and Donelson Confederate General Albert Sydney Johnston realizes he can no longer hold Nashville or any of the ferry boats or bridges along the river. He orders General Hardee to drop back to Nashville, then across the river to safety. General Don Carlos Buell captures Nashville without firing a shot.

February 25.

Congress passes the Legal Tender Act. It allows the government to print paper currency (greenbacks) not backed by an equal amount of specie—gold or silver. This enables the government to pay its bills and finance war spending. By the time the war ends, the government will print $500 million in paper currency—nearly 7 billion dollars in 2019 money.

March 1.

George McClellan begins his ill-fated Peninsular campaign.

March 7.

Confederate General Earl Van Dorn attacks Union forces at Elkhorn Tavern, near Leetown, Arkansas on March 7th. It is the first step in a larger plan to capture Missouri, then make a quick move on Grant.

His troops circle around and attack General Samuel R. Curtis from the rear near Little Sugar Creek at Pea Ridge. Colonel Eugene Asa Carr's men take the brunt of the first attack. General Benjamin McCullough strikes the Union troops on the left outside of Leetown. The fighting is touch and go most of the day. Confederate soldiers outnumber the Union—16,500 to 11,000. The battle for that day ends at dusk, with Confederate General McCullough dead on the field.

March 8.

Confederate troops are tired and low on ammunition. General Earl Van Dorn opens the battle with a cannonade hoping to soften the way for an infantry charge. Union troops respond with their own cannon barrage. After that, Curtis's men charge the rebels and quickly drive them back. Van Dorn's army scatters and disappears into the hills. Pea Ridge ensures that Missouri will remain with the Union.

The battle at Hampton Roads (Virginia) proves the superiority of ironclad boats in naval warfare. The *CSS Virginia* rams the sloop-of-war Cumberland below the waterline, after which she quickly sinks. Next, the *Virginia* and the rest of the Confederate fleet turn their attention to the *USS Congress*. Lieutenant Joseph B. Smith, captain of the *Congress* soon surrenders.

Overnight, the Union ironclad, *Monitor,* rushes to Hampton Roads.

March 9.

The *Monitor* battles the *Virginia* in the first clash of the ironclads.

Both ships give as good as they get. For the most part, the shells bounce harmlessly off their iron sides. At one point, later in the day, the *Monitor* takes a shell to the pilot house. Flying debris momentarily blinds Captain Worden, so the ship pulls out of the battle for a few moments to regroup. Assuming the *Monitor* has decided the fire is too hot, the *Virginia* steams back to Norfolk to effect repairs. When Worden discovers his opponent has left, he returns to his home port.

The ironclads prove themselves in battle. The age of wooden ships is over.

March 13.

Union General John Pope spends two weeks moving up his guns and getting his troops in position to attack New Madrid (Missouri). When he launches his attack on March 14th, he discovers the rebels have abandoned the city.

Pope sets to work digging a bypass canal so that Admiral Foote can get his boats safely to Island Number Ten. Capturing Island Number Ten is the first step in reopening traffic on the Mississippi River.

March 14.

General Ambrose Burnside outnumbers the rebel forces at New Bern (North Carolina), nearly three to one. At first, his thirteen gunboats wait offshore, afraid to cross through the iron spikes sunk in the channel to prevent enemy ships from approaching. Burnside lands his men and launches a full-scale attack on New Bern. As the day progresses, the gunboats run through the barriers and make their way toward shore. When Confederate General Lawrence O'Bryan Branch sees the vessels moving closer, he orders his men to retreat.

March 23.

The Battle of Kernstown (Virginia) stands as Stonewall Jackson's only defeat. His cavalry commander, Colonel Turner Ashby bumps into a large Union force on the 21st. Ashby miscalculates the Union troop strength and tells Jackson they are up against 3,000 men, not the 10,000 that accompany his opponent, General Nathan Kimball.

Jackson's men run out of ammunition and are given orders to withdraw by Brigadier General Richard B. Garnett. When Jackson finds out, he is furious but can do nothing to stop the retreat. Later, he court-martials Garnett for his actions on the field that day.

March 29.

Union troops begin the siege of Fort Macon (North Carolina). The action starts on March 21st when Brigadier General John G. Parke captures four North Carolina cities in five days—Carolina City, Morehead City, Newport, and Beaufort. On March 23rd he sends a message to the commander of the fort offering to parole his men if he turns over the fort. Colonel Moses J. White declines.

Parke lands his men on the Bogue Banks and erects a siege battery to the rear of the fort consisting of two mortar batteries and one thirty-pounder Parrott gun. "There are three naval vessels outside cooperating with us," writes General Ambrose Burnside, "and I hope to reduce the fort within ten days."[7] In the meantime, Burnside decides to place more batteries so he can guard the fort with fewer men as he moves on with his advance along the North Carolina coast.

April 3.

After learning that General Don Carlos Buell is moving his army to join up with Grant, Albert Sydney Johnston orders his men to attack Pittsburg Landing. Johnston's army marches out of Corinth early the next day. The plan is to attack on April 5th, but heavy rain delays the attack until the 6th.

April 6.

A series of battles break out all along the front. Perhaps, the best-known is the Hornet's Nest where Brigadier General Benjamin Prentiss holds his position against eight separate rebel attacks over ten hours. Immediately after the civil war, the fighting at the Hornet's Nest becomes the focus of Shiloh. Everyone says it is the key to the conflict. Today, historians are not so sure.

The battlefield is a confused jumble of soldiers moving forward and backward. General William "Bull" Nelson, from the advance guard of Buell's army, arrives later in the day. General Lew Wallace takes the wrong road and misses the entire first day of fighting.

Somewhere around 2:30, Confederate General Albert Sydney Johnson takes a Minnie ball in his body and another in his leg. He dies shortly, after that.

At the end of the day, Union troops are confined to a three-mile strip along the river's edge. Looking at the battle that night, it seems as if the Confederates are the victors. Grant isn't worried. "We can hold them off until tomorrow," he tells his commanders. "Then they'll be exhausted, and we'll go at them with fresh troops."[8]

April 7.

Grant is right. His army reinforced by Buell's troops and the arrival of Lew Wallace's men fight with a renewed vigor.

The battle opens around seven o'clock. By nine o'clock the roar of the artillery and musketry feels mind-numbing. By early afternoon it is apparent the rebels are retreating towards Corinth. General Hardee says Beauregard issued the order to pull back at one o'clock.[9]

Both sides claim they are the victors. The rebels, because they sustain fewer casualties. The Union because they possess the field at the end of the day.

April 8.

The gunboat Carondelet successfully runs the batteries surrounding Island Number Ten on April 4th. Two days later the Ironclad Pittsburg slips past the batteries. Brigadier General William W. Mackall surrenders Island Number Ten on April 8th. General John Pope captures almost 7,000 prisoners and 123 pieces of field artillery while suffering less than one-hundred casualties.

The action opens the Mississippi River to within fifty miles of Fort Pillow, Tennessee.

April 10.
Captain Quincy A. Gillmore initiates the bombardment of Fort Pulaski (Georgia) after the commander, Colonel Charles H. Olmstead refuses to surrender. His rifled cannon pound away at the fort, damaging the southeast scarp and endangering the shielding over the magazine.

April 11.
Captain Olmstead surrenders Fort Pulaski after surveying the damage to the magazine—worried that many of his men will be killed if it takes a direct hit.

Before the civil war, masonry structures like Fort Pulaski are considered impregnable. Military experts say regular cannon can do little damage to them. "You might as well bombard the Rocky Mountains as Fort Pulaski," quips the army's chief engineer. "The fort could not be reduced in a month's firing with any number of guns of manageable caliber."[10] Rifled cannons change all that. As the reduction of Fort Pulaski proves, modern fortifications are no longer impregnable.

Major General David Hunter acknowledges a radical change in the construction of fortifications is necessary, because "no works of stone or brick can resist the impact of rifled artillery of heavy caliber."[11]

April 16.
The Battle of Lee's Mill is the first of many confrontations in General George McClellan's Peninsular campaign. As battles go, it is more of a skirmish than anything—the Confederates post seven casualties, to the Union's twelve. The rebels position a three-gun battery upstream from the dam, although only one of the guns (a six-pounder) can be brought to play during the fight. After surveying the site, Brigadier General Erasmus Keyes, IV determines, "no part of this line as far as discovered can be taken by assault without an enormous waste of life." McClellan changes his plans and begins a siege on the Warwick-Yorktown line instead.

Abraham Lincoln signs an act that abolishes slavery in the District of Columbia. Congress compensates 2,989 slave owners for their lost property. Lincoln attempted to introduce a similar bill in 1849 when he was a junior congressman from Illinois.

April 19.
Early in 1862 Union forces learn the South is busy constructing ironclads at their naval base near Norfolk, Virginia, so they dispatch General Jesse Reno to destroy the canal connecting the dam to the Pasquotank River. After three hours of stubborn fighting, the rebels run low on ammunition and fall back to Joys Creek. Reno returns to his boats when he learns rebel reinforcements are on the march from Norfolk.

April 25.

The defenses around New Orleans are stripped bare. What remains consists of 3,000 militia, two partially completed ironclads, and a handful of steamboats. Beyond them, are Fort Jackson and Fort St. Phillip. Overnight on April 24th, David Farragut and his fleet of 24 gunboats, 19 mortar boats, and 15,000 men careen past the forts on their way to New Orleans.

Farragut makes short work of the Confederate fleet, sinking eight ships. When General Mansfield Lovell, in charge of the defenses at New Orleans, sees the size of the opposition he has second thoughts about mounting a defense and pulls his troops out of the city.

Union troops begin disembarking that day.

April 26.

General Parke begins the bombardment of Fort Macon (North Carolina). Before doing so, he sends a second request to Colonel White offering to parole his men if he surrenders the fort—intact. White declines—again.

Parke opens a concentrated fire on the fort on April 25th. That combined with a ferocious naval bombardment tears the fort to pieces. White surrenders Fort Macon at dawn the next day. General Burnside paroles his men, allowing them to go home and sit out the remainder of the war.

Union forces control another crucial link along the North Carolina coast.

April 29.
Fort Jackson and Fort St. Phillip surrender, completing the capture of New Orleans.

May 5.
The Battle of Williamsburg (also known as Fort Magruder) is part of McClellan's Peninsular campaign. Confederate forces abandon the fort and continue their withdrawal to Richmond. Both sides sustain heavy casualties—1682 for the Confederates compared to 2283 for the Union.

May 8.
Early in 1862 Confederate General Joseph E. Johnston sends Stonewall Jackson and his foot cavalry into the Shenandoah Valley with orders to prevent Union soldiers there from reinforcing McClellan during his Peninsular campaign. Edward "Alleghany" Johnson attacks the Union troops as they are climbing the western slope of Sitlington's Hill. Johnson outnumbers the Union forces 2800 to 2300 but forfeits much of that advantage by not realizing his men are in open view—making them sitting ducks for the Yankee sharpshooters.

Jackson marches the Stonewall Brigade in the next morning, but he is too late. The Union troops led by Robert H. Milroy slip away overnight.

May 12.

Commander James S. Palmer takes the city of Baton Rouge (Louisiana) without firing a shot. The only protest comes from Mayor B. F. Ryan who says the city will not voluntarily surrender even though there are no soldiers there to defend it. Palmer takes the town without resistance, then steams away to Vicksburg without leaving any troops to guard it. Before leaving, he warns Mayor Ryan that if anyone disturbs the American flag, there will be hell to pay.

May 15.

Drewry's Bluff sits on a 90-foot hillock at a sharp bend in the James River just seven miles outside of Richmond (Virginia). The Union fleet steams around the bend early in the morning. The Galena opens the fight. Four hours later, after fierce fighting, the Union fleet runs low on ammunition. The battle is over.

Commander Rogers orders his ships to turn around. Union forces will not return to Drewry's Bluff for two years.

May 20.

Abraham Lincoln signs off on the Homestead Act. It allows any adult citizen or intended citizen to claim 160 acres of land. The only stipulations are that they must never have borne arms against the United States and that they live on the property for five years, build a home, and plant a minimum of twenty acres. Claimants can speed up the process after six months by paying $1.25 an acre for their land.

Fewer than 15,000 people take advantage of the Homestead Act during the Civil War, but in the years after the war it offers new hope to tens of thousands of Americans and helps to settle the American frontier.

May 23.

Stonewall Jackson attempts to bring about a battle with General Nathaniel Banks at Strasburg. His troops advance up the main valley where he can cross over into the Luray Valley. His cavalry continues up the main valley. If things work out as Jackson hopes, Banks will stop his army long enough for Jackson to slip around and attack Banks' command from the rear.

Instead, Jackson bumps into Colonel John Reese Kenly's force of 1,000 men. Jackson outmans Kenly sixteen to one and soon crushes his small force taking 700 men prisoner.

When Bank learns of the attack, he abandons his position at Strasburg and moves his army toward Winchester. This mini-battle at Front Royal sets Banks up to meet Jackson in a larger confrontation at Winchester the next day.

May 26.

After retreating to Winchester, General Nathaniel Banks positions his troops along Abram's Creek. Fighting breaks out at daylight. Stonewall Jackson attacks Bank's right. When that fails, he moves on the left. The attack breaks Bank's line. Soon, his men are fleeing through the streets of Winchester, with residents shooting at them as they march by.

Jackson pursues them to Stephenson's Depot, then stops. His men need to rest and recuperate. They can't handle anymore fighting.

It is a crushing loss for Nathaniel Banks. He outnumbers Jackson's men almost three to one but suffers more than 2,000 casualties compared to Jackson's 400.

Worse still, by sending Bank's troops to pursue Jackson in the Shenandoah, McClellan loses much-needed manpower for his attack on Richmond.

May 28.

Admiral Farragut's fleet returns to Baton Rouge to find it defended by a small band of rebel guerrillas. After a brief bombardment, he takes control of the city. This time when he steams away, Farragut leaves two gunboats and a small military force under General Thomas Williams to hold the city.

May 30.

General Henry Halleck captures Corinth (Mississippi) without firing a single shot. He later writes his wife, "I have won the victory without the battle." He doesn't bother to chase after General P. G. T. Beauregard's army. To Halleck, capturing strategic vantage points is the way to win the war, rebel armies are not relevant to him.

Abraham Lincoln and Edwin Stanton seem to agree. Two months later they summon Halleck to Washington to take command of the entire army, based primarily on his victory at Corinth.

May 31.

Confederate General Joseph E. Johnston takes advantage of a storm to launch his attack on General George McClellan's troops at Seven Pines (Fair Oaks) Virginia. Union troops stall out on the Chickahominy River, caught in the mud and muck of the spring squall.

Johnston attacks McClellan south of the river, but his inexperienced troops get confused, and his plans go awry. Johnston attacks the next day again but makes no progress. He suffers 6,000 casualties to McClellan's 5,000.

The battle is a turning point in the war, not so much for the fighting, but because Joseph Johnston is injured, and Jefferson Davis appoints Robert E. Lee to take his place as commander of the Army of Northern Virginia. Before that Lee served as a military adviser to Jefferson Davis.

Within the week, Lee changes the rules of the contest when he goes on the offensive launching a string of attacks against McClellan in what becomes known as the Seven Days Battles.

June 4.

General Beauregard orders the defenders of Fort Pillow to abandon the fortifications. After the withdrawal of his army from Corinth, there is no way to protect the fort from a rear attack. Union forces occupy the fort the next day.

June 6.

The Union Navy clashes with a small fleet of Confederate rams above Memphis (Tennessee). They make short work of the rebel fleet, sinking seven out of eight rebel vessels in under two hours.

Federal troops take possession of Memphis which has been largely abandoned by its rebel defenders after the fall of Corinth. Once the railroad is cut off, it becomes impossible for the rebels to supply the city.

June 8.

The Battle of Crosskeys is a minor skirmish fought during the final days of Stonewall Jackson's Shenandoah Valley campaign. A portion of John C. Freemont's army tangles with the advance guard of Jackson's army near Cross Keys Tavern. After exchanging a few volleys, the Union cavalry rejoins their command.

June 9.

The battle at Port Republic (Virginia) is an extension of the Battle of Crosskeys fought the previous day.

Stonewall Jackson's men win the day in heavy fighting, but early in the day, Jackson comes within a hairsbreadth of capture when his men are surprised by advancing Union troops.

Jackson's victories at Crosskeys and Port Republic end his Shenandoah Valley campaign. He marches his troops south to reinforce Robert E. Lee during the Seven Days Battles.

June 25.

Oak Grove is the transitional battle between the end of McClellan's Richmond campaign and the start of the Seven Days Battles.

Union troops advance on the enemy early in the day. They halt for over two hours as McClellan moves forward to take command of the battle. At 1:00 McClellan gives the word to resume fighting. His men surge forward to recover the ground they lost earlier in the action. McClellan trades 1,000 troops for under 600 yards of territory.

June 26.

Robert E. Lee attacks McClellan's army near Mechanicsville (Virginia), along a creek known as Beaver Creek Dam. For Lee's plan to succeed, Stonewall Jackson needs to arrive on time to signal A. P. Hill to launch his attack. Jackson is late. A. P. Hill attacks anyway. The snafu allows McClellan to repulse Lee's attack.

McClellan holds the field but is overcautious and retreats to Gaines's Mill.

June 27.

The battle at Gaines's Mill (Virginia) is touch and go. A rebel soldier says, "I never dreamed of such confusion; our ranks were broken time and again by the fleeing Confederates, really the tide of battle seemed to be madly against us...God only knows how far off were a rout or panic."[12]

Robert E. Lee bets everything on John Bell Hood during the final hours of the battle. Hood pushes his men to the edge of the swamp. Has them fix bayonets. Then at double-quick, they plunge into the swamp screaming the rebel yell.

They overrun the Union defenders. Porter's right and left flanks crumble as those men who survive the rebel onslaught drop their guns and run. The rebels turn their attention to the Union gunners—shooting them down, as the infantry moves on. Johnny Reb captures nine guns, He wants to take more, but the daylight is gone

Lee holds the field as the Union troops retreat. Tomorrow will bring another day of hard fighting.

June 29.

After the battle at Gaines's Mill McClellan begins shifting his men towards Glendale. The 29th finds most of his army at Savage's Station readying themselves to cross White Oak Swamp.

The main attack starts at five o'clock in the afternoon. Although Union forces outnumber the rebels 26,000 to 14,000, they squander the advantage by making piecemeal attacks. The Confederate commander does the same thing, engaging only 10 of his 26 regiments. Still, the fighting is bloody.

Thunderstorms dampen the enthusiasm to fight, and the battle breaks off after dark. Neither side can claim a victory.

June 30.
Just about everything goes wrong for Robert E. Lee at the Battle of Glendale (Virginia). Only James Longstreet and A. P. Hill execute their orders successfully. Stonewall Jackson has orders to rebuild a bridge. When Union artillery and musketry block his way, he lays down to sleep under a tree. Benjamin Huger and John Magruder come under fire and are unable to attack the center.

After dark, Union forces retreat to a stronger position at Malvern Hill, some three miles distant. McClellan is the victor, but both sides suffer a similar casualty rate—3800 for the Union, 3700 for the Confederates.

Strangely enough, George McClellan is not on the field. He has ridden ahead to scout out a new position at Malvern Hill. After the battle, many people will question his motives for leaving the field. Some will suggest he is a coward and moved out of harm's way. The more troublesome aspect is he fails to place anyone in overall command during his absence at Malvern Hill or Glendale.

July 1.

Confederate General D. H. Hill says the Battle of Malvern Hill (Virginia) "was not war. It was murder." He is right. The Union guns tear the Confederate lines apart—repeatedly. They have thirty-six guns mounted on the northern end of Malvern Hill. Twenty and thirty-pound Parrot Rifles sit in reserve on the southern end of Malvern Hill. Add the naval guns, and the rebels don't stand a chance.

In retrospect, Robert E. Lee's forces make a disjointed attack. The artillery batteries act on their own, rather than making a concerted attack. Lee's Generals fight the same way, making piecemeal attacks rather than working a single unified plan.

Malvern Hill is a stunning victory for General George McClellan. Union forces suffered 3,000 casualties to the Confederate's 5,600.

If only McClellan follows up the next day, he could easily chase Robert E. Lee all the way back to Richmond. Instead, he continues his long retreat to Harrison's Landing where his army remains inactive for nearly two months.

For Robert E. Lee the Seven Days Battles are a success and failure. He doesn't deliver a knockout punch to the Union army, but he accomplishes his original goal. He forces the Army of the Potomac to move north—away from the capitol at Richmond.

July 11.

Abraham Lincoln turns over the reins of the army to General Henry Halleck, "Old Brains," and appoints him the new commander in chief. Time will tell whether it is a good or bad decision. Halleck is a genius with paperwork and organization but lacks tactical skills. Like McClellan, he is overcautious and requires time to think everything through. The best Lincoln can say about Halleck is he makes a "first rate clerk."

August 5.

Union troops fight the third battle of Baton Rouge in as many months. This time General John C. Breckinridge, the former vice president of the United States, fresh from Vicksburg with 4,000 Confederate troops spearheads the attack on Williams' army. He expects support from the *CSS Ram Arkansas.*

After six hours of fighting, General Williams is killed. His successor, Colonel Thomas Cahill, is forced back to the river. In this case, retreat is a good thing because it moves the Confederates within range of the Union gunboats. Unknown to Breckinridge, the *Arkansas* falters less than five miles from Baton Rouge and misses the fight.

When the fire from the gunboats grows too intense, Breckinridge gives up on the idea of taking Baton Rouge. He falls back to Comite, then Port Hudson.

August 9.

Cedar Mountain is one of the few battles where the Confederates outnumber Union troops. In this case almost two to one.

Midway through the battle, the Confederate left flank appears to be collapsing. Stonewall Jackson rides into the fray, draws his sword, then attempts to rally his troops. Shortly after that, a desperate last-minute charge by A. P. Hill's Light Brigade swoops in and turns things around.

Union forces make a quick retreat, leaving the rebels victors on the field. Both sides suffer severe casualties—2353 for the Union versus 1338 for the Confederates. Confederate General Charles S. Winder is killed early in the fighting during an artillery barrage.

August 19.

Santee Sioux warriors take advantage of the absence of troops to attack New Ulm (Minnesota), killing 54 people. It is one of the largest Indian attacks ever on an American city. The Sioux make a second attack on August 23rd during which they burn most of the town's structures.

Nearly 400 Indians are taken prisoner, 303 are sentenced to death, and on December 26th the government hangs 39 Santee Sioux warriors in Mankato, Minnesota.

August 28.

The Battle of Groveton (Virginia) is fought the day before the Second Battle of Manassas.

Robert E. Lee orders Stonewall Jackson to capture General John Pope's supply depot at Manassas Junction and cut off Pope's communication with Washington. Jackson accomplishes that task on August 26th. His next mission is to hold Pope's army in place until Robert E. Lee can attack it with the full force of his army.

When he is sure Lee is nearby, Jackson attacks McDowell's third corps near Groveton. The fighting leads into the Second Battle of Bull Run fought over the next two days.

August 29.

The Second Battle of Bull Run takes place just thirty miles outside of Washington, DC. The plan is to move McClellan's army north of Fredericksburg where he can hook up with Pope's army and crush Lee. To counteract that threat, Stonewall Jackson baits John Pope in a series of mini-battles, designed to lead him into a full-scale confrontation with the Army of Northern Virginia. Timing is everything. If Lee is unable to attack Pope before McClellan's army reinforces him his army will be seriously outnumbered.

Assuming he has Jackson trapped, Pope initiates a series of small battles. Jackson repulses each of them.

August 30.
Both sides expect reinforcements. Stonewall Jackson gets an infusion of 28,000 fresh troops from General James Longstreet. The two armies combined, pulverize Pope's army. George McClellan is nowhere to be seen. He decides to keep his troops close to the capitol suspecting an attack is imminent.

The Second Battle of Bull Run delivers a deadly blow to Union forces.

Confederate General Edmund Kirby Smith crushes General William "Bull" Nelson at the battle of Richmond (Kentucky). Everything that can seems to go wrong. The Union right breaks as the men retreat into nearby Rogersville. Nelson rallies his troops in the cemetery, but they can't hold—4300 Union soldiers are taken, prisoner.

September 1.
The Army of Northern Virginia crashes into retreating Union forces at Chantilly (Virginia). Lee's goal is to push the defeated Union army back to Washington, DC. General Isaac Stevens drives the rebel attack back, then takes a bullet in the head and dies. Not long after that, General Philip Kearney loses his direction in a raging thunderstorm and bumps into the Confederate rearguard. He is shot dead.

When he is unable to turn Pope's flank, Robert E. Lee turns his army north—launching his Maryland campaign.

September 4.
General Robert E. Lee begins his disastrous invasion of Maryland. Before engaging in the campaign, he informs Jefferson Davis: "We... must endeavor to harass if we cannot destroy" the Union army. "I am aware that the movement is attended with much risk, yet I do not consider success impossible."

September 5.
General John Pope is relieved of his command, mainly because of his performance at the Second Bull Run. The army banishes him to Minnesota to keep watch on the Sioux Indians there.

September 12.
Union troops stumble across a copy of Robert E. Lee's Special Order 191 wrapped around three cigars. The order gives McClellan an inside look at the Confederate battle plan for the Maryland campaign.

McClellan gets cocky and tells General Gibbon, "Here is a paper with which if I cannot whip Bobby Lee, I will be willing to go home."

September 14.
Union forces face Lee's Army of Northern Virginia in the Battle of South Mountain. It consists of three

separate battles: Crampton's Gap, Turner's Gap, and Fox's Gap. Union troops turn the Confederates back at Crampton's Gap. After stubborn fighting, Lee withdraws his forces from Turner's Gap and Fox's Gap.

September 15.

McClellan's failure to press the rebels after the battle of South Mountain gives Lee time to shift his forces to Harper's Ferry and Antietam. The move dooms Harper's Ferry and allows A. P. Hill the opportunity to march his troops to Sharpsburg on September 17th. He arrives in time to push back Ambrose Burnside's forces as they make their way along the Sharpsburg Road.

McClellan's troops begin arriving in the area of Sharpsburg. McClellan spends all day on the 15th and 16th perfecting his plan of attack.

Mistakenly believing the Confederate forces opposing him outnumber his troops at least two to one, McClellan delays his attack. The next day he orders General Hooker to cross Antietam Creek, seemingly to test the waters while locating a place to launch his attack from on the 17th.

Confederate forces capture the Union arsenal at Harper's Ferry, Virginia. 12,500 Federal soldiers are taken prisoner, the largest number captured in any battle of the civil war.

September 16.

Fighting Joe Hooker crosses Antietam Creek and opens the battle sometime after 4:00 pm. By 10:00 the fighting comes to an end. The men sleep on their arms expecting "the battle for the Republic the next morning."

September 17.

Fighting Joe Hooker launches the battle, this time at the break of dawn. General Ambrose Burnside fights the decisive battle of the day making his way across stone bridge number 3, then fighting his way to Sharpsburg. The arrival of A. P. Hill's troops, fresh from the battle at Harper's Ferry stop his advance. Still, Burnside holds the bridge, something McClellan feels is the key to the fight.

McClellan holds the field but is unsure what the next day will bring.

The fighting at Antietam turns out to be the bloodiest day of the civil war with nearly 23,000 men killed, wounded, and missing on both sides.

September 18th.

No fighting takes place. The two sides call a truce to collect their wounded and bury the dead.

McClellan spends the day planning his next move. Finally, he resolves to resume fighting the following day.

September 19.

Union troops wake up to discover Robert E. Lee has used the cease-fire to move his troops across the Potomac River and back into Virginia.

V Corps led by General Fitz John Porter is the only Union force to chase after the rebels. He attacks the Confederate rear-guard near Boteler's Ford and captures four big-guns. The next day A. P. Hill counterattacks Porter's army and nearly wipes out the 118th Pennsylvania.

The chance to capture the Army of Northern Virginia slips through McClellan's fingers. He determines not to chase after Lee, still convinced the Confederates outnumber his forces.

General Ulysses S. Grant engineers a two-pronged attack on Iuka (Mississippi), sending General Edward Ord by rail, while General William Rosecrans marches his army there. The plan is for the two forces to converge on Iuka. Ord's orders are to wait for Rosecrans to launch his attack, then join the battle when he hears gunfire. A sound anomaly (called an acoustic shadow) prevents Ord from hearing the gunshots, so Rosecrans winds up fighting the battle alone.

General Sterling Price abandons Iuka after dark. Union forces sustained 790 casualties to 1516 for the Confederates.

September 22.

President Lincoln signs the preliminary Emancipation Proclamation. It has more bark than bite because it only frees slaves held in areas occupied by the rebels, so effectively the Emancipation Proclamation doesn't free any slaves. It does renew the Union's purpose for fighting the war and ensures that slavery will no longer exist when the war is over. Lincoln signs the act into law on January 1st, 1863.

October 1.

Abraham Lincoln visits General McClellan's encampment at Antietam to look over the battlefield and to see for himself the state of the army.

October 2.

Early in the morning, Lincoln walks the Antietam battlefield with his old friend Ozias M. Hatch. As they reach the outskirts of the camp, Lincoln shakes his head and points to the nearby army—calling it "General McClellan's bodyguard," a derogatory term he would repeatedly use to describe the Army of the Potomac under McClellan.

October 3.

Confederate Generals Sterling Price and Earl Van Dorn attempt to retake Corinth after losing it to Union forces in May. On the first day of fighting the rebels push Union troops back from rifle pits used in the siege of Corinth.

On the second day of fighting Union troops repulse Confederate forces after fierce hand to hand fighting. General William Rosecrans decides not to chase after the rebel army.

October 8.

The Battle of Perryville is the largest action fought in Kentucky. When it is over, Confederate General Braxton Bragg withdraws his army to Tennessee ensuring that Kentucky will remain in the Union.

October 26.

Almost a month after the Battle of Antietam McClellan moves his troops across the Potomac in a half-hearted attempt to capture the Army of Northern Virginia.

November 7.

Lincoln tires of McClellan's inaction and removes him from command of the Army of the Potomac. He replaces him with General Ambrose Burnside, a man who tells Lincoln three times he is not up to the task. Time will tell, Lincoln should have listened better.

December 7.

While indecisive, the Battle of Prairie Grove (Kentucky) assures that northwest Arkansas, and southwest Missouri will remain with the Union.

December 13.

General Ambrose Burnside leads the Army of the Potomac to battle at Fredericksburg, Virginia. In the ensuing slaughter, the Union suffers 12,653 casualties to 5377 for the Confederates. Everyone agrees it was a good plan, poorly executed.

December 29.

William T. Sherman's army is one part of a two-pronged attack devised by General Grant to take Vicksburg. Sherman moves along the west side of the Mississippi where he is to meet up with Grant outside of Vicksburg. Grant follows along the line of the Mississippi Central Railroad. Nathan Bedford Forrest and Earl Van Dorn destroy Grant's supply depot at Holly Springs. Deprived of those provisions he is unable to meet up with Sherman.

Unaware that Grant is unable to reinforce him, Sherman skirmishes with the rebels for two days then issues an order to storm the fortress. It is an impossible task. One brigade captures a rifle pit but is quickly driven back by heavy fire from above. None of his other troops can cross the open ground. Sherman pulls his men back and contemplates a coordinated attack with navy support from Admiral Porter the next day. It is called off because of dense fog.

December 31.

William Rosecrans's Army of the Cumberland and Braxton Bragg's Army of Tennessee meet at Murfreesboro (Tennessee). The action, known as the Battle of Stones River or the Second Battle of Murfreesboro, rages for three days. Bragg withdraws his army to Tullahoma, Tennessee on January 3, leaving the field to William Rosecrans.

The Union victory at Stones River helps repair some of the psychological damage caused by the disaster at Fredericksburg.

Participants

Confederates

Albert Sidney Johnston.

At the start of the civil war, Albert Sidney Johnston was one of the most respected generals on either side, but the first days of fighting didn't go his way.

Ulysses S. Grant proved a thorn in his side almost from the very beginning. Grant marched into Paducah, Kentucky, the same day the Confederates planned to move on the city. After that, he captured Fort Henry and Fort Donelson, then positioned his army to march into Mississippi.

Johnston concentrated his army around Corinth, Mississippi. Grant inched closer, moving his army to Pittsburg Landing just twenty miles away. Early in April, Johnston learned General Don Carlos Buell's army planned to meet up with Grant, then launch a concentrated attack on Corinth.

On April 3rd, Johnston ordered General P. G. T. Beauregard to attack Grant's army at Pittsburg Landing before the two armies could hook up. It might have worked—except for the weather. It stormed so bad on April 4th that it slowed the army's progress, so they could not attack until the 6th. That allowed Buell to arrive in time for the second day of the fighting.

Johnston died early in the fighting on the first day. Later, Jefferson Davis would say Johnston's death was "the turning point of our fate." It shows the faith he placed in his old West Point classmate, but it also makes one wonder—Did Davis have doubts about the war's outcome, almost from the beginning?

Grant had reservations about Albert Sidney Johnston. He didn't "question the personal courage of General Johnston or his ability." While "he did not win the distinction predicted for him by many of his friends," wrote Grant. "He did prove that as a general he was overestimated."[13]

General P. G. T. Beauregard.

Gustave Pierre Toutant-Beauregard taunted Union forces through much of the conflict. He launched the first battle of the civil war when he ordered his artillery to attack Fort Sumter on April 14th, 1861.

Again, at the first Bull Run, Beauregard and General Joseph Johnston led the attack on General Irvin McDowell's Union army. At one point, Beauregard grabbed a regimental battle flag and rode among his troops urging them to fight on.

Beauregard argued with Albert Sidney Johnston before the battle. He thought they should call it off. They had planned to attack on the 4th, but because of weather and personnel delays, they couldn't get into position until the morning of the 6th. Beauregard believed that had cost them the element of surprise they were counting on to get an edge on Grant. Johnston decided to continue with the attack.

Beauregard assumed command at Shiloh after the death of General Albert Sidney Johnston. Despite having Union troops confined to a 3/4-mile strip along the shore at the end of the day, Beauregard delayed launching a second offensive until the next morning. That allowed Grant to reinforce his lines with the troops of Lew Wallace, William "Bull" Nelson, and Don Carlos Buell.

In his official report of the battle, Beauregard said his troops moved forward like an "Alpine avalanche..." They took "nearly all of his field artillery, about 30 flags, colors, and standards; [and] over 3,000 prisoners."

Early the next morning, the battle "raged with a fury which satisfied me I was attacked by a largely superior force." The Confederates repulsed each charge, but the Federal troops came back as if reinforced after each repulse. "About 1 pm, I determined to withdraw," wrote Beauregard, "from so unequal a conflict."[14]

Braxton Bragg.

Braxton Bragg was one of the most controversial generals in the Confederacy. As a young officer out of West Point, he picked quarrels with his superiors—a habit he kept up throughout his military career. Many of his biographers talk about what a burden it was to write about such a man. Don Seitz said Bragg was "a much-hated man whose military efforts led to defeat." Stanley

Horn said that Bragg was unpopular "with practically everyone he encountered."

Timothy Smith said the terrain around Shiloh unnerved Bragg. He didn't like "fighting a battle on ground that he did not know well."[15]

In his official report of the battle, Bragg cursed everything. The commanders were deficient, "the equipment was lamentably defective for field service," and their transportation was "defective."[16]

He said they were given orders to attack on the morning of the 5th, but that was impossible. "About 2 am a drenching rainstorm commenced, to which the troops were exposed, without tents, and continued until daylight." The men at the front of their line kept up a continuous fire throughout the night despite orders to the contrary. "Under such circumstances little or no rest could be obtained by our men."[17]

The next morning, "the enemy did not give us time to discuss the question of attack, for soon after dawn he commenced a rapid musketry fire on our pickets." As the day wore on, Bragg found "military spoils of every kind. The enemy was driven headlong from every position and thrown in confused masses upon the riverbank, behind his heavy artillery and under cover of his gunboats at the Landing. He left nearly the whole of his light artillery in our hands and some 3,000 or more prisoners."[18]

That night "the commanders found it impossible to find or assemble their troops." In the morning, they found themselves "confronting a large and fresh army, which had arrived during the night." Gradually, they were pushed back and made an orderly retreat to Corinth.[19]

Leonidas Polk.

Leonidas Polk had to have one of the oddest backstories in the civil war. At the time Jefferson Davis tapped him to serve as a general, he was an Episcopal Bishop in Tennessee. Polk had virtually no military experience, other than having attended West Point (and being Jefferson Davis's classmate) many years before.

At the beginning of the war, Kentucky took a hands-off approach to the war. Governor Beriah Magoffin warned Union and Confederate forces not to set foot in Kentucky. In September 1861, Leonidas Polk committed a military faux pas by sending troops to occupy Columbus, Kentucky. That move more than anything made Kentucky side with the Union.

At Shiloh Polk agreed with the other commanders that the weather prevented them from attacking on the 5th. The roads were "exceedingly bad in consequence of the heavy rain which had fallen," His men kept bumping into Braxton Bragg's troops who were clogging the road.[20]

The next day, General Beauregard told him they would need to "forego the attack" because their "success depended in surprising the enemy [and] that was now impossible." Johnston soon overrode Beauregard and scheduled the attack for the next morning.[21]

At the end of the first day, victory seemed assured. We "were with 150 to 400 yards of the enemy's position," wrote Polk, "and nothing seemed wanting to complete the most brilliant victory of the war but to press forward and make a vigorous assault on the demoralized remnants of his [Grant's] forces."[22]

What stopped absolute victory that day was the gunboats. They gave the rebel soldiers the impression that "our forces were waging an unequal contest; that they were exhausted and suffering from a murderous fire." And then, just as suddenly, the rebel forces were withdrawn by General Beauregard.[23]

Polk has little to say about the second day at Shiloh, other than they were ordered to withdraw from the field at 2:30.

William J. Hardee.

William J. Hardee was a career military officer with the United States Army and the Confederate States Army. He attended West Point, spent two years studying at the prestigious French Cavalry School at Saumur, France. From 1856 to 1860, he served as commandant of cadets at West Point. In 1855 he published a manual on *Rifle and Light Infantry Tactics*, better known as *Hardee's Tactics*.

In his official report of the battle, General Beauregard commended Hardee for "the zeal, intelligence, and energy with which all orders were executed." He added, "Major General Hardee was slightly wounded, his coat rent by balls and his horse disabled."

Today, Hardee is remembered for the "Hardee Hat," the regulation dress hat of the civil war.

John C. Breckinridge.

If it hadn't been for the war, John C. Breckinridge might have been president of the United States. He served as vice president under James Buchanan, campaigned for president in 1860, and in 1861 was appointed a Kentucky senator. After Kentucky sided with the union, Breckinridge fled to the south.

In November 1861 he took command of the "Orphan Brigade," made up mostly of Kentuckians who felt abandoned after that state declared for the Union.

The Orphan Brigade lost nearly a third of their men at Shiloh. On the first day of fighting, they caged General Prentiss up at the Hornet's Nest, so he'd be forced to surrender. The next day they stood firm near Shiloh Church so that the others could make good on their escape. "This was hard duty," said Colonel R. P. Trabue, "exposed as the command had been and wasted as they were by the loss of half their numbers."[24]

Union

Ulysses S. Grant.

Ulysses S. Grant was an unknown quantity coming into the civil war. He'd been drubbed out of the service in the 1850s for being overly fond of drink, had failed at every civilian occupation he tried, and back in the army—his reputation as a drunkard followed him.

When the war broke out, he presented himself to Governor Richard Yates of Illinois. Yates didn't know what to make of him. He said Grant's, "appearance at first is not striking...He was plain, very plain."[25] That's what everyone would say throughout the war. Grant stood a little better than five foot nothing, weighed in at a hundred and thirty pounds, and tended to blend in with the scenery. At his first official visit to Washington, Lincoln asked Grant to stand on a sofa so people could get a better look at him.

In September 1861, after a little prodding from Congressman Elihu Washburne, Lincoln appointed Grant, a brigadier general of volunteers headquartered in Cairo, Illinois.

From there, the legend grew.

Six days after arriving at Cairo, Grant loaded his men on the Steamer *Mound City* and set off to capture Paducah, Kentucky. After that, he made a somewhat disastrous attack on Belmont, Missouri. Starting in February 1862, Grant launched a miraculous string of victories. His army captured Fort Henry and Fort Donelson in Tennessee, which led Confederate General Albert Sidney Johnston to pull his troops out of Tennessee. No shots were fired as General William "Bull" Nelson marched his forces into Nashville following close on the heels of the retreating rebels.

Now, General Ulysses S. Grant waited outside of Pittsburg Landing, poised to take Shiloh, Corinth, Richmond, then the Confederacy.

William T. Sherman.
Like Grant, Sherman's career fluttered up and down before the civil war. After leaving the military, he became a banker in San Francisco. When his bank failed, he moved to Kansas City and practiced law; then he became headmaster of a military school in Louisiana.

Sherman reentered the service at the start of the civil war. After Bull Run, Lincoln promoted him to brigadier general of volunteers. His next position with the Army of the Cumberland in Tennessee was the low point of Sherman's military career. He grew paranoid about how small and unprepared his army was and called for 200,000 troops to support him.

Soon, the newspapers were having a field day labeling Sherman crazy or insane.

For a while, it looked like his career was over. *The New York Herald* reported Sherman wasn't insane, but "he certainly acted strangely when he was in Kentucky... he has been known for many years as extremely eccentric man and liable to all sorts of freaks of judgment." The *Herald* felt safe in saying Sherman would "never have an important command again."[26]

Two months later, Sherman was back in the field serving with Grant at Fort Donelson and then at Shiloh.

While Sherman proved his bravery at Shiloh, his troops were among the first to turn and run.

He defended them as best he could. "My division was made up of regiments perfectly new," explained Sherman, "nearly all having received their muskets for the first time at Paducah. None of them had ever been under fire or beheld heavy columns of an enemy bearing down on them...To expect of them the coolness and steadiness of older troops would be wrong."[27]

When he recollected Pittsburg Landing in his memoirs, Sherman defended Grant for not building intrenchments. "The battle of Shiloh, or Pittsburg Landing," said Sherman, "was one of the most fiercely contested of the war."[28] The reason they hadn't dug in was simple. They never figured Beauregard would leave his fortifications at Corinth. General Grant planned to force the rebels out once Buell's army arrived.

Don Carlos Buell.

Don Carlos Buell was somewhat of a hothead. In his early years at Jefferson Barracks, he was court-martialed for drawing his sword during an argument and slicing off a portion of the man's ear. He fought in the Mexican War, then worked in the adjutant general's office for the next fourteen years.

At the start of the civil war, he helped George McClellan train the Army of the Potomac. Buell took command of the Army of Ohio in November 1861 and marched into Nashville, Tennessee early the next year. In

March, Henry Halleck ordered him to move his army to Pittsburg Landing to assist Grant in taking Corinth. His army arrived at Pittsburg Landing late in the afternoon on the first day of fighting and contributed to the victory on the second day.

Looking back on the battle, Buell believed Grant was responsible for the near defeat on the first day. When Buell's army arrived, there was no "line or order of battle, no defensive works of any sort, no outposts, properly speaking, to give warning, or check the advance of an enemy, and no recognized head during the absence of the regular commander." That allowed the enemy to sneak up on Grant's army, and almost destroy it.[29]

Buell pretty much took credit for ending the fighting on the first day. "A reinforcing army [Buell's Army of Ohio] arrived on the opposite bank of the river, crossed, and took position under fire at the point of attack; the attacking force was checked, and the battle ceased for the day."[30]

What offended Buell most, was Sherman and Grant made it sound as if the Army of Ohio was "an unnecessary intruder in the battle."

Lew Wallace.

Wallace's career after the civil war was more impressive than anything he accomplished during the war. As Governor of the New Mexico Territory, he brokered a deal with Billy the Kid to turn himself in after the Lincoln County Wars, then thought the better of it.

About that same time, he completed writing his bestselling novel, Ben Hur. Much later, it would be turned into a motion picture starring Charlton Heston.

Lew Wallace was with Ulysses S. Grant's army almost from the start. He fought with him at Fort Henry and performed so well at Fort Donelson that he was promoted to major general.

Shiloh was a different story. Early in the morning, Grant sent Captain A. A. Baxter to order Wallace to march immediately to Pittsburg Landing. When Wallace did not show up by one o'clock, Grant dispatched Colonel McPherson and Captain Rowley to find him. As it turns out, Wallace took the wrong road and missed the entire first day of fighting.[31]

In his official report, Grant questioned Wallace's choice of roads. "General Lewis Wallace, at Crump's Landing, 6 miles below, was ordered at an early hour in the morning to hold his division in readiness to move in any direction to which it may be required. At about 11 o'clock the order was delivered to move it up to Pittsburg but owing to its being led by a circuitous route did not arrive to take part in Sunday's action."

The mix up would haunt Wallace for the remainder of his military career.

William "Bull" Nelson.

There was a reason they called General William Nelson—Bull. He was a monster of a man. He stood six foot four, weighed over three hundred pounds and had a sharp, biting tongue.

Before the civil war, Nelson had spent most of his time at sea in the United States Navy. He graduated from the Naval Academy at Annapolis, rising to the rank of lieutenant. Early in 1861 he teamed up with Abraham Lincoln's old friend, Joshua Speed, and distributed 5,000 guns to Union supporters in Kentucky.

In mid-September 1861 Nelson was appointed a brigadier general in the Union army. He led the advance division of Don Carlos Buell's army to Pittsburgh Landing, and on the second day was in the thick of the fighting.

Three weeks later, William "Bull" Nelson lay dying on the floor of the Galt House Hotel—shot down by Jefferson Davis. Not the Confederate president, but Union General Jefferson C Davis. Nelson insulted him earlier in the month, and when he wouldn't apologize Davis intended to force him. Later, he said it was an accident, but no one was sure. Davis never apologized or expressed any regret for the killing.

John A. McClernand.

McClernand's fellow generals considered him a bit of a braggart. "We did the fighting, he did the writing," commented Richard Oglesby.[32] He was one of those political generals like John Pope and Benjamin Butler, who received and kept their positions, because of the political clout they had back home, rather than their skills on the battlefield.

After the battle of Shiloh, McClernand took the liberty of writing Abraham Lincoln: "My division, as usual, has borne or shared in bearing the brunt... I have lost in killed and wounded about every third man of my command. Within a radius of two hundred yards of my headquarters, some 150 dead bodies were left on the field."[33]

At one point he ordered his division to fall back on the landing. "This was my sixth line. Here we rested a half hour, continuing to supply our men with ammunition until the enemy's cavalry were seen rapidly crossing the field to charge. Waiting till they approached within some thirty paces of our line, I ordered a fire, which was delivered with great coolness and destructive effect." The enemy "turned and fled in confusion, leaving behind a number of horses and riders dead on the field."[34]

Sunday night, his men rested on their arms in the drenching rain. The next day McClernand was back in the thick of the fighting. "Here one of the severest conflicts ensued that occurred during the two days. We drove the enemy back and pursued him with great vigor to the edge of the field... Our position at this moment was most critical, and a repulse seemed inevitable." What saved them was reinforcements from General Thomas' Louisiana Legion. "Extending and strengthening my line, this gallant body poured into the enemy's ranks one of the most terrible fires I ever witnessed." The enemy broke their ranks and "fell back in disorder."[35]

Ending his missive to the president, McClernand suggested Grant and Buell messed up by not pursuing the enemy "on Monday night and Tuesday."[36]

W. H. L. Wallace.

The story of the Hornet's Nest is most often tied up with W. H. L. Wallace and Benjamin Prentiss. Wallace died late in the fighting leaving Prentiss the last general standing, so General Benjamin Prentiss became the hero of Shiloh.

That may, or may not, be the case.

Prentiss started the day with several thousand mainly green, untested troops. As the rebels surged towards them, most of his men skedaddled back towards the landing. About 500 of them stayed, and they made their stand on the sunken road near W. H. L. Wallace's troops. Later he was reinforced by 575 men of the 23rd Missouri who came up from the Landing.

Early in the morning, Grant made his rounds and ordered Prentiss to hold his position at all costs, and he did—up until about 5:30.

That's when General Daniel Ruggles turned up the heat on the Hornet's Nest. He ordered James C. Thrall to "concentrate as much artillery as possible at this point, to prevent General Prentiss from being reinforced from the river..." It was extremely effective. "The reinforcements that were going to the relief of General Prentiss, not being able to withstand the shower of shot, shell, and shrapnel that was poured upon them, fell back in confusion towards the river, which resulted in the surrender of General Prentiss, with his division."[37]

Wallace died about 5:00. A half hour later, Prentiss raised the white flag and surrendered his 2200 men, "at 5:30, when finding that further resistance must result in the slaughter of every man in the command, I had to yield the fight."[38]

When the battle ended, W.H. L. Wallace's actions at the Hornet's Nest faded into the background. Prentiss was the hero. He was the man everyone associated with the deadliest fighting at Shiloh.

Even though General W. H. L. Wallace initiated the fighting there and was present longer than Prentiss, he has become the forgotten man. If he is mentioned at all, it is usually as a footnote to the action at the Hornet's Nest—and then, only to say, he died in the fighting.

Stephen A. Hurlburt.

Stephen A. Hurlburt was another one of those political generals that confounded Lincoln and Grant throughout the war. None of them had a lick of military sense or training, but they had enough political clout back home to keep Lincoln from removing them. The best Grant could do was work around them. After the midterm elections in 1862, he was able to remove some of them after Lincoln's re-election in 1864 Grant had free reign to remove them.

The *Davenport Democrat and News* said Hurlburt was one of many "self-elected political hacks and ambitious placeholders" who were incompetent as soldiers.[39] The *Carrollton Press* went a step further and said, "Hurlburt is known to be an intemperate man... during the late session of the Legislature, it was the rule with him to be drunk by the middle of the afternoon." Making him a general incurred a "strong risk of bringing shame upon the fair fame of our state."[40]

Perhaps, his major contribution at Shiloh was helping the navy target its artillery on the gunboats Lexington and Tyler. He told Captain Gwin, of the navy, to fire "on the position on the left of my campground and open fire as soon as our fire was within that line." From his "observation and the statement of prisoners his fire was most effectual in stopping the advance of the enemy on Sunday afternoon and night."[41]

Pittsburg Landing, or the Battle of Shiloh

Pittsburg was your typical riverboat landing. It stood in the middle of nowhere where the Tennessee River spreads out over one hundred yards wide. Off to the east, there is nothing but marshland and forests. The landing itself sits on the west bank. There were no houses or buildings (other than two simple log huts). Its significance was it stood at the point where the road from Corinth intersected with the river making it easy for the rebels to land and transport supplies.

The Union army pitched their camp at Pittsburg Landing. The rebels waited at Corinth, roughly twenty miles distant. Corinth formed the junction of several major railroads in the Mississippi Valley. One ran east to Memphis; the other traveled south into the heart of Dixie. A third railroad connected Corinth with Jackson, Tennessee.

Grant lined his troops up in a semi-circle running from Lick Creek on the left to Owl Creek on the right. The flood waters protected the army's rear. One result of this was the rebels could only attack from the front. Grant did not need to worry about which direction an attack would come from.

The rebel troops were stationed behind strong fortifications at Corinth. It never occurred to Grant that the Confederates would come out from behind their breastworks to attack him. He figured he would need to draw them out.

Better intelligence would have helped Grant here. Time was ticking off for the Confederates. When General Albert Sydney Johnston learned General Don Carlos Buell's army was getting ready to meet up with Grant, he decided to dislodge Grant immediately. "On Thursday, April 3, the Army of the Mississippi was ordered to advance from Corinth to Shiloh."[42]

General William T. Sherman's troops made their camp at what would become the epicenter of the battle near Shiloh, a small wooden church located two or three miles outside of Pittsburg Landing. General McClernand's forces held the position to Sherman's left and rear. To McClernand's left was Prentiss, and then Stuart. General Charles F. Smith's brigade was stationed to the right of Sherman—held in reserve until needed.

On Friday night, two days before the battle, General Sherman's pickets bumped into a Confederate reconnaissance party. That sparked a heated exchange of fire for some time. Several soldiers playing euchre in the woods got caught in the crossfire One unlucky trooper got killed instantly. Another had three fingers shot off his hand.[43]

The firing afterward lasted for hours, but nothing came of it. Sherman had orders from General Grant not to "bring on an attack," so the pickets eventually pulled back.[44] Sherman, like Grant, did not expect Beauregard to attack. It made more sense for him to "chose ground as far back from our stores as possible."[45]

The Confederates marched up from Corinth on April 4th. They had planned to attack early the next morning, but a storm the previous night made that impossible. It turned the roads into muck and mud that stopped all travel. As a result, none of the troops were able to get into position.

A reporter from the *Chicago Daily Tribune* was nearby in General McClernand's camp when fighting broke out early Sunday morning, April 6th. He said they heard shots coming from the direction of Sherman's camp, but not enough to make it seem like "anything important" so they sat down to breakfast. At half-past seven wounded men began to pour in from Sherman's hospitals. They said they had come under heavy fire during the attack and the hospitals were moving to the rear.

McClernand marched his troops out at double-quick speed to reinforce Sherman. When McClernand's troops came up, they stood on a ravine that overlooked the Union camp. They could see the rebel troops looting Sherman's tents.

Colonel Smith of the Lead Mine regiment opened fire on the rebels. Then, Major Smith drew his saber and led the charge calling out, "Go in, boys. Give them some more Galena pills. They'll think they opened a new lead mine."

When they ran out of ammunition, the Galena men fixed their bayonets and charged. The enemy turned and ran.[46]

The fighting that day was fierce. Grant thought the rebel assault showed a "disregard of losses on their side."[47] He would later be accused of the same thing when newspapers began to call him a "butcher"[48] and Lincoln the "widow maker"[49] after the Battles at the Wilderness and Cold Harbor.

There were other smaller battles fought at Shiloh on those two days—Fallen Timbers, Widow Bell's Cotton Field, and the Peach Orchard to name a few, but the fight at the Hornet's Nest has come to symbolize the actions that took place there.

General Prentiss was in the thickest of the fighting almost from the start.

His division and General W. H. L. Wallace's division positioned themselves in a field near what is now called the Sunken Road. The rebels attacked them continuously for nearly ten hours. The Minnie balls whizzed by the men like hornets rushing out of their nests.

Early in the day on Sunday, Grant visited Prentiss and ordered him to "maintain his position" at the Sunken Road "at all hazards."[50] F. Quinn, Colonel of the Twelfth Michigan Infantry, said Prentiss held his position from nine o'clock to half-past four "amid the most dreadful carnage for a little space ever witnessed on any field of battle during this war."[51]

Lt. Col. Quin Morton, of the Twenty-Third Missouri Infantry, said they were forced to change position several times. By four o'clock the enemy had outflanked them. Several times they pushed the rebels back, but Johnny Reb charged again and again. At half-past five they were "surrounded and fired upon from front and rear by two batteries and infantry." Still, Prentiss tried to break through.[52]

Even the Confederates admired his spunk. S. S. Heard, Colonel of the Seventeenth Regiment Louisiana Volunteers, reported that by one o'clock they had carried all the enemy encampments except Prentiss'. "For two hours our success at that point appeared doubtful."[53]

By midafternoon the battle could have gone either way.

Prentiss held his own as reinforcements continued to strengthen his position. Then about four o'clock, General Daniel Ruggles' Battery concentrated a heavy fire on Prentiss' position that prevented more reinforcements from reaching him.

That proved effective. The men going to reinforce Prentiss turned and ran towards the river rather than face the "shower of shot, shell, and shrapnel" thrown at them.[54]

After General W. H. L. Wallace was mortally wounded his men pulled back leaving Prentiss alone on the field. Prentiss fought like a wildcat, but by half-past five, "finding that further resistance must result in the slaughter of every man in the command," he said, "I had to yield the fight."[55] Prentiss surrendered his force of 2200 men.

That was on the first day of fighting at Shiloh.

Immediately after the Civil War, the fighting at the Hornet's Nest became the focus of Shiloh. Everyone talked about it as the key to the conflict. Today, historians are not so sure that's accurate. They acknowledge the action at the Hornet's Nest bought Grant the precious time he needed to regroup and turn the battle around. As far as the Hornet's Nest being the key to Shiloh, that's open to debate.

The same goes for Prentiss' action that day. Early in the fighting, his troops dwindled from 5400 to 500 as his frightened soldiers fled from the rebels along the Sunken Road. Not long after that, reinforcements arrived from W. H. L. Wallace's division.

Some historians say Prentiss became the hero of the Hornet's Nest because he was the last man standing. General W. H. L. Wallace received a mortal wound. Colonel Peabody died early in the day. Because they couldn't tell their stories, Prentiss's report was taken as Gospel. He became the *Hero of the Day*.

Grant and Sherman had plenty of warnings a rebel attack was imminent. Union pickets bumped up against Confederate pickets daily. Shots were exchanged often, but no one considered it more than enemy reconnaissance missions—sometimes in force.

On Friday, April 4th, Sergeant C. J. Eagler spotted a large force of rebels in front of Company B. Eagler said he and Samuel Tracey walked to the edge of a plantation. "There we saw the enemy in force, and to all appearances, they were getting breakfast. We saw infantry, cavalry, and artillery very plainly."[56] When Sherman found out, he "ordered him [Eagler] put under arrest for bringing a false alarm into camp."[57]

Sherman did not believe the report. He dismissed the rebel sighting as nothing more than a scouting party in force.

Later that day, Colonel Ralph P. Buckland's pickets captured a dozen rebel prisoners. Several of them admitted they were part of a larger Confederate force dispatched to take Pittsburg Landing. Again, Sherman ignored the warning. Like Grant, he believed the rebels would never come out from behind their fortifications at Corinth.

William "Bull" Nelson, of Buell's command, marched his troops into Savannah on the morning of April 5th. He'd busted his ass rushing his men from Nashville to Pittsburg Landing and was anxious to get his men in position before the battle started. Nelson was taken completely off guard when Grant told him the soonest; he could get him to Pittsburg Landing was Tuesday, April 8th.

If Grant had paid more attention to the early warning signals emanating from Shiloh, Nelson's men could have made the difference on April 6th.

The fighting started just after two o'clock that morning when Colonel Peabody from Prentiss' Division set out with four-hundred men to scout the area directly ahead of them. Less than half a mile from camp Peabody's scouts encountered a large force of Confederates and came under heavy fire.

At six o'clock that morning all hell busted out along Sherman's lines. By half-past eight o'clock the fighting had spread across the entire front. The *Cincinnati Times* correspondent said thousands of stragglers clogged the roads. For many of them, this was their first taste of battle. From the looks of things, they did not find it "much to their liking." The stragglers drifted toward the river, and "neither persuasion or threats could induce them to change their course."[58]

"Foot by foot the ground was contested." By the end of the day, "a single narrow strip of open land dividing the opponents" was all the ground the Union had left. The sound of artillery and musket fire was deafening. Men fell in bloody piles. The men behind them stepped over their fallen bodies as they would walk over fallen logs.

The gunboat Tyler made its way upriver and joined in the fighting early in the afternoon. "The shell went tearing and crashing through the woods, felling trees in their course and spreading havoc everywhere they fell."[59] The gunfire from the ship helped check the rebel advance on the left.

At five o'clock the rebel fire ceased for a moment as they fell back to their center. Then just as quick, they wheeled about and attacked the left wing with all their forces. About that same time, General Buell's command arrived. Grant directed the gunboats Tyler and Lexington to a position a half-mile above Pittsburg Landing where they let loose a terrible and murderous cannonading. Not long after that, General Lew Wallace's troops arrived at the landing.

That convinced General Beauregard to call it quits for the day. The rebels slowly fell back to their center on the Corinth road.

Grant called the fighting "a case of Southern dash against Northern pluck and endurance." Most of the troops were raw. Many "were hardly able to load their muskets according to the manual." The officers were no better than their men. Grant understood why several regiments turned and ran. Only the colonels who marched their men off the battlefield at the first sound of gunfire were "Constitutional cowards" in his eyes.[60]

Sherman's troops were raw and untested. They were among the first to turn and run. That did not surprise anyone. Many of them had just got their guns a few days before. Several Ohio regiments dropped their weapons and fled to the rear, notably Colonel Appler's 53rd Ohio.

Andrew F. Davis of the 15th Indiana Infantry Regiment, Company I, watched everything unfold. He noted in his diary, "Several regiments of the Ohio Troops and one of the Iowa Regts. took a regular stampede and made a most cowardly retreat."[61]

When Grant rode back to the river to meet with Buell he estimated there were four or five thousand "stragglers lying under the cover of the river-bluff, panic-stricken, most of whom would have been shot where they lay, without resistance, before they would have taken up muskets and marched to the front to protect themselves."[62] He did not seem worried, or anxious to get them back to the front.

Cowardice wasn't unique to the Union army. On Monday, Colonel Moore's Second Texas Regiment "broke and fled disgracefully from the field."[63]

For the regular soldiers, it was just another day's fighting. Sherman described the rebel attack as a "beautiful, dreadful sight."[64] He had at least five close calls with the Grim Reaper on the first day. His soldiers reported seeing him all over the battlefield, urging his men on and helping to sight artillery. To many of his soldiers, it appeared Sherman had a death wish.

In his official report of the battle, Grant commended Sherman. He said, Sherman "displayed great judgment and skills in the management of his men." Grant noted Sherman got wounded in the hand the first day of fighting, wounded again later in the day, and had three horses "killed under him."[65]

All the commanders experienced close calls. Lieutenant Colonel McPherson had a horse shot out from under him. Captain Carson got his head blown off by a cannonball while riding next to General Grant.[66]

Confederate General Albert Sidney Johnston died at half-past two. "One of his legs was torn by a shell, and a Minnie ball struck him in the body." General Beauregard assumed command of the army on his death.[67] Grant didn't believe Johnston's wound was so bad. He thought Johnston died because he didn't take care of his injury. He bled to death rather than leave his men alone on the battlefield.[68]

The *Evening Star* joined several other papers in rumormongering and speculation. They reported General Beauregard "had his arm shot off."[69] That eventually proved untrue as did the rumor Beauregard had been killed during the battle. The truth was he received a "slight wound" in his left arm.[70]

The correspondent for the *Cincinnati Commercial* reported, "Each man fought as if success or defeat depended upon his own right arm, and charge after charge was made upon the Rebels to regain the ground we had lost.

"They stood firm as a rock, and though our artillery often swept down their ranks, and left fearful gaps in their columns, they manifested no trepidation, nor did they waver for a moment.

"The living supplied the place of the dead. The musket that had fallen from a lifeless hand was seized at once. Hand-to-hand struggles were innumerable. Every struggle was for life. Quarter was asked on neither side, and the ground drank up the blood of hundreds of brave fellows every hour."

The correspondent thought the men "lost all semblance of humanity." All he could see was the "spirit of the demon" in their faces.[71]

Defeat followed every success. The rebels pushed ahead then gave way to the Union advances. Then the Union advanced only to fall back. The men were nothing more than "wild beasts." Powder and smoke filled the air. "Arms, legs, and heads were torn off" as the troops advanced into the melee."[72]

The fighting on April 6th "raged with a fury that defies description." At five o'clock the rebels temporarily ceased their fire. Then, just as quickly the fight was back on. "The gunboats Tyler and Lexington poured in their shot thick and fast, with terrible effect."[73]

Andrew Davis stepped off a steamboat at Pittsburg Landing around one o'clock on Sunday afternoon. "The Minnesota, Pennsylvania, Kentucky, Illinois, and Indiana troops contested every inch of ground during the whole day," he said, "but were compelled to gradually fall back." By nightfall, the Union men were crammed into a tiny strip no more than three-quarters of a mile wide. Surrender appeared imminent. "Had it not been for the river," Davis was sure, "it would have been a worse stampede than Bull Run ever was."

The next day when he reached the battlefield, "the enemy were in full retreat."

A quarter of a mile from the landing he saw his first dead body. "In many places, they lay so thick that a person could step from one to another for many rods. In one place I counted seven rebels piled on top of each other where they had stood at their cannon and fought." There were bodies with the "head entirely shot away," another one was "cut entirely in two." Others had "their legs or arms shot off," and still others were "so mangled that it would be almost impossible to tell that they had ever been a human being."[74]

Despite losing ground on the first day, General Grant felt confident he could turn things around. "We can hold them off until tomorrow," he told his commanders. "Then they'll be exhausted, and we'll go at them with fresh troops."[75] Buell's army arrived at close to five o'clock. Too late to help on the first day, but a welcome addition for the next day's battle.

Lew Wallace finally made it up with his five thousand troops. Grant couldn't help feeling Wallace's absence was a big part of the problem on Sunday. Early in the morning, Grant sent Captain A. A. Baxter to order Wallace to march immediately to Pittsburg Landing. When Wallace did not show up by one o'clock, Grant dispatched Colonel McPherson and Captain Rowley to find him. As it turns out, Wallace took the wrong road and missed the entire first day of fighting.[76]

A heavy thunderstorm rolled in after midnight. That and the continued cannonading from the gunboats kept the men awake most of the night.

Grant ordered his division commanders to throw out skirmishers early in the morning.

The battle opened around seven o'clock on the morning of April 7th. By nine o'clock the roar of the artillery and musketry was mind-numbing. The firing from the Union line "was as steady as clockwork." The "roar of the battle shook the earth."[77]

General Nelson's men crossed the river early and fell in on the left flank. General Buell's troops arrived at the landing at about eleven o'clock. They marched up the hill and took a position on the right near General Wallace's command.

The Union guns shook the earth throwing cannonballs into the rebel positions. Taylor's Chicago Battery poured volley after volley of canister into an open field known as the "Battalion Drill Ground" near Sherman's command. It tore into the rebels leaving death and destruction at every turn.

The second day did not go as well for the Confederates. Colonel R. G. Shaver of the Seventh Arkansas Infantry reported a "terrific and murderous fire" opened upon them that compelled them to fall back. "Disorder and confusion prevailed."[78]

A rebel soldier said they "drove the Federals from hill to hill and from ravine to ravine all day long. We exhausted our cartridges time and again and continued on with the bayonet...the dead were piled up on every field by the hundreds, with the most-ghastly looking wounds you ever looked at. Most of the Yankees that I saw dead were shot through the head, and their brains had oozed out on the ground."[79]

By early afternoon it was apparent the rebels were retreating towards Corinth. General Hardee said Beauregard gave the order to pull back at one o'clock.[80]

General Beauregard claimed the victory because the rebels sustained fewer casualties than the Federal troops, but the *Evening Star* was not so sure.

"Was it a defeat?" they asked. "Certainly not. If a man attempts to knock me down and the matter ends in my knocking him down, I'm not defeated."[81] Later the paper added, "Certainly it was not a defeat. But was it a decisive victory?" In the end, they did not have enough information "to form a satisfactory opinion."[82]

General Grant estimated the Union loss at 1,500 killed and 3,500 wounded. He believed the rebel loss was much higher. The animals took it just as hard. Two hundred horses died in the fighting.[83]

The uproar over the alleged misconduct of Grant and Sherman roared as intensely as the battle. Everyone had an opinion. No one had proof.

Stories circulated about Sherman and Grant not taking enough care at Pittsburg Landing and Shiloh. Some observers thought they should have had their pickets out farther in advance to prevent a surprise attack.

General Don Carlos Buell felt Grant and Sherman were a bunch of bunglers who nearly lost their armies. When he arrived at Pittsburg Landing the command there "had no line or order of battle, no defensive work of any sort, no outposts...and no recognized head during the absence of the regular commander."[84] Buell believed Grant's army was a disaster waiting to happen. His account of the battle at Shiloh published in *Century Magazine's, Battles and Leaders of the Civil War,* implied Grant and Sherman doctored their accounts of the battle to negate the element surprise paid in their near defeat on the first day of the battle.[85]

Sherman dismissed those reports in a letter to his brother John. The newspaper reports, "as usual," were made "by people who ran away and had to excuse their cowardice by charging bad management on the part of leaders." In Sherman's opinion, it was petty jealousy mixed with overzealous news reporters.[86]

In another letter to his brother, John, in December, Sherman displayed the same disdain for reporters. "I allow no reporters about."[87] This time, it was for security. "The enemy shall learn nothing of my forces, plans or purposes, through an egotistical and corrupt press."[88]

Looking back on the battle twenty-five years later, Grant described Shiloh as constantly misunderstood."[89] He didn't see any need to defend his conduct. "As to the talk about a surprise here, nothing could be more false. If the enemy had sent us word when and where they would attack us, we could not have been better prepared. Skirmishing had been going on for two days between our reconnoitering parties and the enemy's advance lines. I did not believe. However, they intended to make a determined attack, but were simply making a reconnaissance in force."[90]

No matter. The papers were for and against him.

The *Muscatine Weekly Journal* (Iowa) wrote, "General Buell, and not General Grant, is the real hero of Pittsburg Landing." His timely arrival saved the army from a total defeat by Beauregard. The paper ended its rant calling Grant "a pompous charlatan" whose name had "no magic for the soldier."[91]

The New York Herald agreed. Buell "arrived at the critical moment and saved the fight." That did not stop them from complimenting Grant. They said, "by his enduring heroism Grant held the enemy at bay until Buell arrived." That made it sound like Grant was a faithful puppy dog waiting for his master to return. It was a compliment, but... Finally, they got to the point. "Such a man deserves something more than censure."[92]

If anything, it proved the papers were like the politicians and the people—opinionated, uninformed, and willing to make snap judgments before they had all the facts.

In short, they were human and willing to be swayed by crazy bullshit.

The *Cincinnati Commercial* started a rumor Sherman and Prentiss had been taken entirely by surprise at the start of the battle. The article said, "many guns were unloaded, accouterments lying pell-mell, ammunition was ill supplied—in short, the camps were completely surprised—disgracefully."[93] The reporter went on to say many of the men were killed in their sleep or shot while emerging from their tents. "Officers were bayoneted in their beds," then left there to fester in their gore for two days while the battle raged.[94]

The National Republican repeated and embellished that same rumor in the Capitol. "The beginning of the fight on that day [April 6th] was a total surprise, many officers, and soldiers being overtaken in their tents and slaughtered or taken prisoner."[95]

The funny thing is, the Confederate leaders on the ground that day never talked about marching in and catching Sherman and Grant with their pants down. General Hardee said the enemy attacked the skirmishers in front of his lines at daybreak on April 6th. In less than a half-hour, the action escalated into a fierce battle.

The initial advance proved deadly for the rebels. By Hardee's estimates, the Sixth Mississippi "lost more than 300 killed out of an effective force of 425 men."[96]

Hardee's report doesn't make it sound like the element of surprise played any part in the battle. If it had, he would have talked about the number of Union troops slaughtered, not about three out of four members of one of his regiments being cut down.

The battles at Fort Donelson and Shiloh were just the beginning. Each ensuing battle saw fiercer, more desperate fighting, and casualties no one could have imagined at the beginning of the war. In a few short years, the death and destruction at Shiloh would seem inconsequential compared to the losses suffered at Antietam, Gettysburg, and Petersburg.

The Civil War was a game changer. It altered the way the world looked at war.

Cincinnati Gazette Account

*(This dispatch is the gold standard for war reporting. It covers the entire battle on Sunday and Monday, describing troop positions casualties, etc. The report is biased against Grant and Sherman, and it is the account that launched the rumors about the camps being taken unaware—of men being slaughtered as they sleep. Read it with caution. Double check your facts, if in doubt. Overall, it is an accurate factual account of the Battle of Shiloh. It was originally printed in the **Cincinnati Gazette**. This account was reprinted in the **New York Herald**. April 16, 1862.)*

Correspondence of the Cincinnati Gazette
Field of Battle
Pittsburg Landing
April 9, 1862.

Fresh from the field of the great battle, with its pounding and roaring of artillery, and its keener voiced rattle of musketry still sounding in my wearied ears; with all its visions of horror still seeming seared upon my eyeballs, while scenes of panic-stricken rout and brilliant charges, and obstinate defenses, and succor, and intoxicating success are burned alike confusedly and indelibly upon the brain, I essay to write what I know of the battle of Pittsburg Landing.

Yet, how bring order out of such a chaos? How deal lastly, writing within twenty-four hours of the closing of the fight, with all the gallant regiments of the hundred present that bravely won or as bravely lost, and with all that ignobly fled in panic from the field? How describe, as that one man may leisurely follow the simultaneous operations of a hundred and fifty thousand antagonists, fighting backward and forward for two long days, in a five-mile line and over four-mile retreat and advance, under eight division commanders on one side, and an unknown number on the other? How, in short, picture on a canvass so necessarily small a panorama so grandly great? The task is impossible.

But what one man, diligently using all his powers of observation through those two days, might see, I saw, and that I can faithfully set down. For the rest, after riding carefully over and over the ground, asking questions innumerable of those who know, and sifting consistent truth from the multiplicity of replies with whatever skill some experience may have taught, can only give the concurrent testimony of the actors.

The Situation Before the Battle

Our great Tennessee expedition had been up the river some four weeks. We had occupied Pittsburg landing for about three weeks; had destroyed one railroad connection, which the rebels had restored in a day or two and had failed in a similar but more important attempt on another. Beyond this we had engaged in no active operations. The rebels, alarmed by our sudden appearance, began massing their troops under our eyes. Presently they had more in the vicinity than we had. Then we waited for Buell, who was crossing the country from Nashville by easy marches. The rebels had apparently become restive under our slow concentrations, and General Grant had given out that an attack from them seemed probable. Yet we had lain at Pittsburg Landing, within twenty miles of the rebels that were like to attack us in superior numbers, without throwing up a single breastwork or preparing a single protection for a battery, and with the brigades of one division stretched from extreme right to extreme left of our line, while four other divisions had been crowded in between as they arrived.

On the evening of Friday, April 4, there was a preliminary skirmish with the enemy's advance. Rumors came into camp that some of our officers had been taken prisoners by a considerable rebel force, near our lines, and that pickets had been firing. A brigade, the Seventieth, Seventy-second and Forty-eighth Ohio regiments, was sent out to see about it. They came upon a party of rebels, perhaps a thousand strong, and after a sharp little action drove them off, losing Major Crocket, of the Seventy-second Ohio, and a couple of Lieutenants

77

from the Seventieth, prisoners, taking in return some sixteen, and driving the rebels back to a battery they were found to have already in position, at no great distance from our lines. General Lew Wallace's troops, at Crump's Landing, were ordered out under arms, and they marched to Adamsville, halfway between the river and Purdy; to take position there and resist any attack in that direction. The night passed in dreary rain, but without further rebel demonstration; and it was generally supposed that the affair had been an ordinary picket fight, presaging nothing more. Major General Grant had indeed said there was great probability of a rebel attack, and there was no appearances of his making any preparation for such an unlooked-for event, and so the matter was dismissed. Yet on Saturday there was more skirmishing along our advanced lines.

The Rebel Designs

There can be no doubt the plan of the rebel leaders was to attack and demolish Grant's army before Buell's reinforcements arrived. There were rumors that such a movement had been expressly ordered from headquarters at Richmond, as being necessary as a last bold stroke to save the failing fortunes of the Confederacy in the West, though of that no one, I presume, knows anything.

But the rebel leaders at Corinth were fully aware that they largely outnumbered Grant, and that no measure had been taken to strengthen the position at Pittsburg Landing; while they knew equally well that when Buell's entire Kentucky army arrived, and was added to Grant's forces, they could not possibly expect to hold their vitally important position at Corinth against us. Their only hope, therefore, lay in attacking Grant before Buell arrived, and so defeating us in detail. Fortunately, they timed their movements a day too late.

The Warning of Danger

The sun never rose on a more beautiful morning than that of Sunday, April 6. Lulled by the general security I had remained in pleasant quarters at Crump's, below Pittsburg Landing, on the river. By sunrise I was roused by the cry. "They're fighting above." Volley, of musketry could sure enough be distinguished, and occasionally the sullen boom of artillery came echoing down the stream. Momentarily the volume of sound increased, till it became evident that it was no skirmish that was in progress, and that a considerable portion or the army must be already engaged. Hastily springing on the guards of a passing steamboat. I hurried up.

The sweet spring sunshine danced over the rippling waters, and softly lit up the green of the banks. A few fleecy clouds alone broke the air above. A light breeze murmured among the young leaves; the bluebirds were singing their gentle treble to the stern music that still came louder and deeper to us from the bluffs above.

And the frogs wore croaking their feeble imitation from the marshy islands that studded the channel.

Even thus early the west bank of the river was lined with the usual fugitives from action hurriedly pushing onwards, they know not where, except downstream and away from the light. An officer on board hailed them and demanded their reason, but they all gave the same response: "We're clean cut to pieces, and every man must save himself."

At the lauding appearances became still more ominous. Our two Cincinnati wooden gunboats, Taylor and Lexington, were edging uneasily up and down the banks, eager to put in their broadsides of heavy guns, but unable to find where they could do it. The roar of battle was startlingly close and showed that the rebels were in earnest attempt to carry out their threat of driving us into the river. The landing and bluff above were covered with cowards who had fled from their ranks to the rear for safety and who were telling the most fearful stories of the rebel onset and the sufferings of their own regiments.

Momentarily, fresh fugitives came back often guns in hand, and all giving the same accounts of thickening disasters in front

Hurrying out toward the scene of action, I was soon convinced that there was too much foundation for the tales of the runaways. Sherman's and Prentiss' entire divisions were falling back in disorder, sharply pressed by the rebels in overwhelming numbers, at all points.

McClernand's had already lost part of its camps, and it too, was falling back. There was one consolation—only one—I could see just then: History, so the divines may say, is positive that no attack ever made on the Sabbath was eventually a success to the attacking party. Nevertheless, the signs were sadly against the theologians.

Let me return—premising that I have thus brought the reader into the scene near the close of the first act in our Sunday's tragedy—to the preliminaries and the opening of the assault.

Topographical Position of Our Troops

And first, of our positions. Let the reader understand that the Pittsburg Landing is simply a narrow ravine, down which a road passes to the river bank, between high bluff on either side There is no town at all. Two log huts comprise all the improvements visible. Back from the river is a rolling country cut up with numerous ravines, partially under cultivation, but perhaps the greater part thickly wooded with some underbrush. The soil is clayey, and the roads on Sunday morning were good. From the Landing a road leads direct to Corinth, twenty miles distant. A mile or two out this road forks; one branch is too lower Corinth road, the other the ridge Corinth road. A short distance out, another road takes off to the left, crosses Lick creek, and leads back to the river at Hamburg, some miles further up. On the right, two separate roads lead off to Purdy, and another, a new one, across Snake creek to Crump's Landing on the river below. Besides these, the whole country inside our lines is cut up with roads leading to our different camps; and beyond the lines is the most extricable maze of cross roads, intersecting everything and leading everywhere, in which it was ever my ill fortune to become entangled.

On and between these roads, at distances of from two to four or five miles from Pittsburg Landing, lay five divisions of Major General Grant's army that Sunday morning. The advance line was formed by three divisions. Brigadier General Sherman's—Brigadier General Prentiss' and Major General McClernand's. Between these and the Landing lay the two others—Brigadier General Hurlburt's and Major General Smith's, commanded, in the absence (from sickness} of that admirable officer, by Brigadier General Lew Wallace.

Our advance line, beginning at the extreme left, was thus formed—on the Hamburg road, just this side the crooking of Lick Creek and under bluffs on the opposite bank that commanded the position, lay Colonel D. Stuart's brigade of General Sherman's division. Some three or four miles distant from this brigade, on the lower Corinth road, and between that and the one to Purdy lay the remaining brigades of Sherman's division, McDowell's forming the extreme right of our whole advance line, Hildebrand's coming next to it, and Buckland's next. Next to Buckland's brigade, though rather behind a portion of Sherman's, lay Major General

McClernand's division and between it and Stuart s brigade, already mentioned as forming our extreme left, lay Brigadier General Prentiss division, completing the line.

Back of this line, within a mile of the landing, lay Hurlburt's division, stretching across the Corinth road, and W. H. L. Wallace's to his right. Such was the position of our troops at Pittsburg landing at daybreak on Sunday morning. Major General Lew Wallace's division lay at Crump's landing, some miles below, and was not ordered up till about half-past seven o'clock that day.

It is idle to criticize arrangements now—it is so easy to be wise after a matter is over—but the reader will hardly fail to observe the essential defects of such arrangements. Nearly four miles intervened between the different parts of Sherman's division. Of course, to command the one he must neglect the other. McClernand's lay partially behind Sherman and therefore, not stretching far enough to the left, there was a gap between him and Prentiss, which the rebels did not fail speedily to find. Our extreme left was commanded by unguarded heights, easily approachable from Corinth, and the whole was confused and ill-adjusted.

The Rebel Plan of Attack

During Friday and Saturday, the rebels had marched out of Corinth, about seventy thousand strong, In three great divisions. Sidney Johnston had general command of the whole army, and particularly of the center. Braxton Bragg and Beauregard had the wings. Hardee, Polk, Breckinridge, Cheatham and others held subordinate commands. On Thursday Johnston issued a proclamation to the army, announcing to them in grandiloquent terms that he was about to lead them against the invaders, and that they would soon celebrate the great, decisive victory of the war, in which they had repelled the invading column, redeemed Tennessee and preserved the Southern confederacy.

Their general plan of attack is said by prisoners to have been to strike our center first (composed, as the reader will remember, of Prentiss' and McClernand's divisions), pierce the center, and then pour in their troops to attack on each side the wings into which they would thus cut our army.

To accomplish this, they should have struck the left of the three brigades of Sherman's division which lay on our right, and the left of McClernand's, which came to the front on Sherman's left. By some mistake, however, they struck Sherman's left alone, and that but a few moments before a portion of their right wing swept up against Prentiss.

Troops First Attacked

The troops thus attacked, by six o'clock, or before it, were as follows: The left of Sherman's brigades, that of

Colonel Buckland, was composed of the Seventy second Ohio, Lieutenant Colonel Canfield, commanding; Forty-eighth Ohio, Colonel Sullivan; Seventieth Ohio, Colonel Cockerell, and Fifty-third Ohio, Colonel Appler.

To the right of this was Colonel Hildebrand's brigade, Seventy-seventh Ohio, Lieutenant Colonel commanding; Fifty-ninth Ohio, Colonel Pfyffe, and the Fifty-third Illinois. And on the extreme right, Colonel McDowell's brigade, Sixth Iowa (Colonel McDowell—Lieutenant Colonel commanding; Fortieth Illinois, Colonel Hicks; Forty-sixth Ohio, Colonel Thomas Worthington.

General Prentiss' division was composed of the Twelfth Michigan. Sixteenth Wisconsin, Eighteenth Wisconsin, Eighteenth Missouri, Twenty-third Missouri, Twenty-fifth Missouri, and Sixty-first Illinois.

The Battle on Sunday

Almost at dawn Sherman's pickets were driven in, a very little later Prentiss' were; and the enemy were into the camps almost as soon as were the pickets themselves.

Here began scenes, which let us hope, will have no parallel in the remaining annals of the war. Many, particularly among our officers, were not yet out of bed. Others were dressing, others washing, others cooking, a few eating their breakfasts. Many guns were unloaded, accoutrements lying pell-mell, ammunition was ill-supplied—in short, the camps were completely surprised—disgracefully, might be added, unless someone can here after give some yet undiscovered reason to the contrary—and were taken at almost every possible disadvantage.

The first wild cries from the pickets rushing in, and the few scattering shots that preceded their arrival aroused the regiments to a sense of their peril; an instant afterwards rattling volleys of musketry poured through the tents, while, before there was time for thought or preparation, there came rushing through the woods, with lines of battle sweeping the whole fronts of the division camps and bending down on either flank, the fine, dashing. compact columns of the enemy.

Into the just aroused camps thronged the rebel regiments, firing sharp volleys as they came, and springing forward upon our laggards with the bayonet, for while their artillery, already in position, was tossing shells to the further side of the encampments, scores were shot down as they were running, without weapons, hatless, costless, toward the river. The searching bullets found other poor unfortunates in their tents, and there, all unheeding now, they still slumbered, while the unseen foe rushed on. Others fell as they were disentangling themselves from the flaps that formed the doors to their tents; others as they were buckling on their accoutrements; others as they were vainly trying to impress on the cruelly exultant enemy their readiness to surrender.

Officers were bayoneted in their beds and left for dead, who, through the whole two days' fearful struggle, lay there gasping in their agony, and on Monday evening were found in their gore inside their tents, and still able to tell the tale.

Such were the fearful disasters that opened the rebel onset on the lines of Buckland's brigade, in Sherman's division. Similar, though perhaps less terrible in some of the details, were the fates of Prentiss' entire front.

Meantime, what they could our sheltered regiments did. Falling rapidly back through the heavy woods till they gained a protecting ridge, firing as they ran, and making what resistance men thus situated might, Sherman's men succeeded in partially checking the rush of the enemy long enough to form their hasty line or battle. Meantime, the other two brigades of the division (to the right) sprang hastily to their arms and had barely done so when the enemy's lines came sweeping up against their fronts, too, and the battle thus opened fiercely along Sherman's whole line on the right.

Buckland's brigade had been compelled to abandon their camps without a struggle. Some of the regiments, it is even said, ran without firing a gun. Colonel Appler's Fifty-third Ohio is loudly complained of on this score, and others are mentioned. It is certain that parts of regiments, both here and in other divisions, ran disgracefully. Yet they were not wholly without excuse. They were raw troops, just from the usual idleness of our "camps of instruction," hundreds of them had never heard a gun fired in anger; their officers, for the most part, were equally inexperienced; they had been reposing in fancied security, and were awaked, perhaps, from sweet dreams of home, and wives, and children, by the stunning roar of cannon in their very midst, and the bursting of a bombshell among their tents—to see only the serried columns of the magnificent rebel advance, and through the blinding, stilling smoke, the hasty retreat of comrades and supports, right and left. Certainly, it is sad enough but hardly surprising, that under such circumstances some should run. Half as much caused the wild panic at Bull Run, for which the nation, as one man became a loud-mouthed apologist.

But they ran—here as in Prentiss' division, of which last more in a moment—and the enemy did not fail to profit by the wild disorder. As Buckland's brigade fall back McClernand threw forward his left to support it. Meanwhile Sherman was doing the best to rally his troops—dashing along the lines, encouraging them everywhere by his presence, and exposing his own life with the same freedom with which he demanded their offer of theirs, he did much to save the division from utter-destruction. Hildebrand and McDowell were compelled to retire their brigades from their camps across the little ravine behind, but here, for a time they made a gallant defense, while what was left of Buckland's was falling back in such disorder as it might, and leaving McClernand's left to take their place, and check the wave of rebel advance.

Capture of General Prentiss

General Prentiss was faring scarcely to well. Most of his troops stood their ground, to be formed into line but, strangely enough, the line was drawn up in an open space, leaving to the enemy the cover of the dense scrub oak in front, from which they could pour in their volleys in comparative safety.

The men held their position with an obstinacy that adds new laurels to the character of the American soldier; but it was too late. Down on either flank came the overwhelming enemy. Fiercely pushed in front, with a wall of bayonets closing in on either side like the contracting iron chamber of the Inquisition, what could they do but what they did? Speedily their resistance became less obstinate, more and more rapidly they fell back, less and less frequent became their returning volleys.

The enemy pushed their advantage. They were already within our lines; they had driven one division from all its camps, and nearly opened, as they supposed the way to the river. Just here, between nine and ten o'clock, McArthur's brigade of W. H. L. Wallace's division came up to give some assistance to Stuart's brigade of Sherman's division, on the extreme left, now in imminent danger of being cut off by Prentiss' defection. McArthur mistook the way, marched too far to the right, and so, instead of reaching Stuart, came in on the other side of the rebels, now closely pushing Prentiss. His men at once opened vigorously on the enemy, and for a time they seemed likely still to save our imperiled division. But coming unawares, as they seem to have done, upon the enemy, their positions were not well chosen, and all had to fall back together.

Brigadier General Prentiss and three regiments with him—the Twenty-third Missouri, of his own division, and the Twelfth and Fourteenth Iowa, of those that had come to his assistance—delayed their retreat too long. Almost before they were aware of their danger, the flanking forces rushed in from either side behind them, and they stood, perhaps two thousand strong, in the midst of thrice their number. They threw down their arms, and the rebels signaled their first attack by marching three Lincolnite regiments, with a division general, as prisoners, to their rear.

Overwhelmed by this fresh disaster, without a general to organize them, with still hotter and hotter fire to their front and flanks, the remainder of the division, whole regiments at a time, gave way in disorder. For a short time, a few maintained a confused defense, retreating, baiting, firing, courting death by remaining in isolated squads or companies, to resist a little longer the overpowering advance; but before ten o'clock the whole division was in rapid retreat. Some regiments came off the field in a degree of order; the most in sad confusion.

And, thus by ten o'clock one entire division of our army was hors de combat. A deep gap in our front line was made, the rebels had nearly pierced through, and were only held back by McArthur's brigade, and the rest of W. H. L. Wallace's division which hurried over to its assistance.

For the present let us leave them there. They held the line from this time on till four.

Sherman's Division – McClernand's

We left Sherman's brigades maintaining a confused fight, Buckland's about gone, Hildebrand's and McDowell's holding their ground more tenaciously. The firing aroused McClernand's division. At first they supposed it to be a mere skirmish; perhaps even only the irregular discharge of muskets by guards and pickets, to clean out their guns, a practice which, to the disgrace of our discipline be it said, was well-nigh universal, and rendered it almost impossible at any time to know whether firing meant anything at all, beyond ordinary disorder of our own soldiers. But the continued rattle of musketry soon undeceived them, and almost as soon the advance of the rebels pouring after Buckland was upon them.

The division, it will be remembered, lay a short distance in the rear, and with one brigade stretching out to the left of Sherman's line. Properly, speaking merely from the location of the camp, McClernand did not belong to the front line at all. Two-thirds of his division were entirely behind Sherman. But as the latter fell back, McClernand had to bare the shock of battle.

His division was composed as follows: First brigade, Colonel Hare commanding, Eighth and Eighteenth Illinois, Eleventh and Thirteenth Iowa; Second brigade, Colonel C. C. Marsh commanding. Eleventh, Twentieth, Forty-eighth and Forty-fifth Illinois, Colonels Ransom, Marsh, Haynie and Smith (the latter is the Lead Mine regiment); Third brigade, Colonel Raitt commanding, Seventeenth, Twenty-ninth and Forty-ninth Illinois, Lieutenant Colonels Wood, Farrell and Pease, and Forty-third Illinois, Colonel Harsh. Besides this one show of experienced troops they had Schartz's, Dresser's, McAllister's and Waterhouse's batteries.

As already stated, McClernand was first called into action shortly after the surprise of Sherman's left brigade (Buckland's) about seven in the morning—by having to move up his left brigade to support Sherman's retreating left and preserve the line. Then, as Sherman's other brigades fell back, McClernand's moved up and engaged the enemy in support.

Gradually the resistance in Hildebrand's brigade and what was still left to its right of Buckland's, became more confused and irresolute. The line wavered, the men fell back in squads and companies, they failed to rally promptly at the call of their officers. As they retreated the woods behind them became thinner and there was less protection from the storm of grape that swept as if on blasts of a hurricane among the trees. Lieutenant Col. Canfield, commanding the Seventy-second Ohio, was mortally wounded and borne dying from the field.

Colonel Sullivan, of the Forty-eighth Ohio, was wounded, but continued at the head of his men. Company officers fell and were carried away from their men. At one of our wavering retreats, the rebels, by a sudden dash forward, had taken part of Waterhouse's battery, which McClernand had sent them over. Beer's battery, too, was taken, and Taylor's Chicago Light Artillery was so terribly pounded as to be forced to retire with heavy loss. As the troops gave way they came out from the open woods into old fields, completely raked by the enemy's fire. For them all was lost, and away went Buckner's and Hildebrand's brigades, Ohioans and Illinoisans together, to the rear and right, in such order as they might.

McDowell's brigade had fallen back less slowly than its two companions of the same division, but it was now left entirely alone. It had formed our extreme right, and of course had no support there; its supporting brigades on the left had gone; through the space they had occupied the rebels were pouring; they were in imminent danger of being entirely cut off, and back they fell too, still farther to the right and rear, among the ravines that border Snake creek.

And here, so far as Sunday's fight is concerned, the greater part of Sherman's division passed out of view. The General himself was indefatigable in collecting and reorganizing his men, and a straggling contest was doubtless kept up along portions of his new lines, but with little weight in inclining the scales of battle. The General bore with him one token of the danger to which he had exposed himself—a musket ball through the hand. It was the general expression of all that his escape so lightly was wonderful. Whatever may be his faults or neglects, none can accuse him of a lack of gallantry and energy when the attack was made on his raw division that memorable Sunday morning.

Attack on McClernand's Right

To return to McClernand's division. I have spoken of his sending up first his left and then his center brigade to support Sherman, shortly after the surprise. As Sherman fell back, McClernand was compelled to bring in his brigades again to protect his left against the onset of the rebels, who seeing how he had weakened himself there, and inspired by their recent success over Prentiss, hurled themselves against him with tremendous force. To avoid bringing back these troops, a couple of new regiments, the Fifteenth and Sixteenth Iowa, were brought up; but taking utterly raw troops on the field, under heavy fire, was too severe a trial for them, and they gave way in confusion. To meet the attack, then the whole division made a change of front, and faced along the Corinth road. Here the batteries were placed in position, and till ten o'clock the rebels were foiled in every attempt to gain the road.

But Sherman having now fallen back, there was nothing to prevent the rebels from coming in farther out on the road and turning McClernand's right. Prompt to seize the advantage, a brigade of them went dashing audaciously through the divisions abandoned camp, pushing up the road to come in above McClernand, between where him and Sherman had been. Dresser's battery of rifled guns opened on them as they passed, and with fearful slaughter—not confined, alas! to one side only drove them back.

But the enemy's reserves were most skillfully handled, and the constant advance of fresh regiments was at last too much for our inferior numbers. Major Eaton, commanding the Eighteenth Illinois, was killed; Colonel Haynie was severely wounded; Colonel Raitt, commanding a brigade, had his leg so shattered that amputation was necessary; Major Nevins, of the Eleventh Illinois, was wounded; Lieutenant Colonel Ransom, of the same regiment, was wounded; three of General McClernand's staff—Major Schwartz, Major Stewart and Lieutenant Freeman—were wounded, and carried from the field. Line officers had suffered heavily. The batteries were broken up. Schwartz had lost half his guns and sixteen horses. Dresser had lost several of his rifled pieces, three caissons and eighteen horses. McAllister had lost half his twenty-four-pound howitzers.

The soldiers fought bravely to the last—let no man question that—but they were at a fearful disadvantage. Gradually they began falling back, more slowly than had Prentiss' regiments, or part of Sherman's, making more determined, because better organized resistance, occasionally rallying and repulsing the enemy in turn for a hundred yards, then being beaten back again, and renewing the retreat to some new position for fresh defense.

By eleven o'clock the division was back in a line with Hurlburt's. It still did some gallant fighting; once its right swept around and drove the enemy for a considerable distance, but again fell back, and at last it brought up near the position of W. H. L. Wallace's division.

We have seen how Prentiss, Sherman and McClernand were driven back; how, fight as fiercely as they would, they still lost ground; how their camps were all in the hands of the enemy; and how this whole front line, for which Hurlburt and Wallace were but the reserves, was gone.

The Assault on Sherman's Left

But the fortune of the isolated brigade of Sherman's division, on the extreme left, must not be forgotten. It was doubly left alone by the generals. General Grant did not arrive on the field until after nearly all these disasters had crowded upon us, and each Division General had done that which was good in his own eyes, and carried on the battle independent of the rest; but this brigade was even left by its Division General, who was four miles away, doing his best to rally his panic-stricken regiments there.

It was commanded by Colonel David Stuart (of late Chicago divorce case fame, and ex-Congressman), and was composed of the Fifty-fifth Illinois, Lieutenant Colonel Malmbourg, commanding; Seventy-first Ohio, Colonel Rodney Mason; the Fifty-fourth Ohio (Zouaves), Colonel T. K. Smith. It was posted along the circuitous road from Pittsburg Landing, up the river to Hamburg, some two miles from the landing, and near the crossing of Lick creek, the bluffs on the opposite side of which commanded the position and stretching on down to join Prentiss' division on its right. In selecting the grounds for the encampment of our army, it seems to have been forgotten that from Corinth an excellent road led direct to Hamburg, a few miles above this left wing of our forces. Within a few days, the oversight had indeed been discovered, and the determination had been expressed to land Buell's forces at Hamburg, when they arrived, and thus make all safe. It was unfortunate, of course, that Beauregard and Johnston did not wait for us to perfect our pleasing arrangements.

When the rebels marched out from Corinth, a couple of brigades (rumored to be under the command of Breckinridge), had taken this road, and thus easily, and without molestation reached the bluffs of Lick creek, commanding Stuart's position.

During the attack on Prentiss, Stuart's brigade was formed along the road, the left resting near the Lick Creek ford, the right, Seventy-first Ohio, Colonel Rodney Mason, (late Assistant Adjutant General of Ohio, and Colonel of the Second Ohio at Manassas,) being nearest Prentiss. The first intimation they had of disaster to their right was the partial cessation of firing. An instant afterwards muskets were seen glinting among the leaves, and presently a rebel column emerged from a bend in the road, with banners flying and moving at double-quick down the road toward them. Their supports to the left were further off than the rebels, and it was at once seen that, with but one piece of artillery a single regiment could do nothing there. They accordingly fell rapidly back toward the ford and were reinforced in an orchard near the other regiments.

The rebel column veered on further to the right, in search of Prentiss' flying regiments, and for a brief space, though utterly isolated, they were unmolested.

Before ten, however, the brigade, which had still stood listening to the surging roar of battle on the left, was startled by the screaming of a shell that came directly over their heads. In an instant the batteries of the rebel force, that had gained the commanding bluff opposite, by approaching on the Corinth and Hamburg road, were in full play, and the orchards and open fields in which they were posted (looking only for attack in the opposite direction) were swept with the exploding shells and hail-storm rush of grape.

Under cover of this fire from the bluffs, the rebels rushed down, crossed the ford, and in a moment were seen forming this side the creek, in open fields also, and within close musket range. Their color bearers stepped defiantly to the front, as the engagement opened furiously, the rebels pouring in sharp and quick volleys of musketry, and their batteries above continuing to support them with a destructive fire. Our sharpshooters wanted to pick off the audacious rebel color bearers, but Colonel Stuart interposed, "No, no, they are too brave fellows to be killed." Almost at the first fire, Lieutenant Colonel Barton S. Kyle, of the Seventy-first, was shot through the breast. The brigade stood for scarcely ten minutes, when it became evident that its position was untenable, and they fell rapidly back, perhaps a quarter of a mile, to the next ridge; few of his men, at great personal risk, carrying Lieutenant Kyle in a dying condition, from the field they were abandoning. Ohio lost no braver, truer man, that day.

As they reached the next woody ridge, rebel cavalry, that had crossed the creek lower down, were seen coming up on their left, and to resist this new attack the line of battle was formed fronting in that direction for three quarters of an hour the brigade stood here. The cavalry, finding its purpose foiled, did not come within range. In front they were hard pressed, and the rebels, who had followed Prentiss began to come in on their right. Colonel Stuart had sent across to Brigadier General W. H L. Wallace, then not engaged, for support Brigadier General McArthur's brigade was promptly started across, but mistaking the way, and bearing too much to the right, it speedily found itself in the midst of the rebel forces that had poured in after Prentiss. General McArthur could thus render Stuart's brigade no assistance, but he vigorously engaged the rebels to his front and flanks, fell back to a good position and held these troops in bay till the rest of his division came up to his aid. General McArthur was himself disabled by a wound in the foot, but he rode in to a hospital, had it dressed and returned to his brigade, which meantime sturdily held its position.

But this brought Stuart's isolated brigade little help. They were soon forced to fall back to another ridge, then to another, and finally, about twelve o'clock, badly shattered and disordered, they retreated to the right, and rear, falling in behind Gen. McArthur's brigade to reorganize. Colonel Stuart was himself wounded by a ball through his right shoulder, and the loss of field and company officers was sufficient to greatly discourage the troops.

Desperate Condition of National Troops

This clears our entire front line of divisions. The enemy has full possession of all Sherman's, Prentiss's, and McClernand's camps. By ten o'clock our whole front, except Stuart's brigade, had given way, and the burden of the fight was resting on Hurlburt and W. H. L. Wallace. Before twelve Stuart, too, had come back, and for the time absolutely only those two divisions stood between our army and destruction or surrender.

Still all was not lost. Hurlburt and Wallace began making a most gallant stand, and meantime most of the troops from the three driven divisions were still to some extent available. Many of them had wandered to the river—some as far as Crump's Landing and some even to Savannah. These were brought back again on transports. Lines of guards were extended to prevent skulkers from getting back to the landing, and especially to stop the shrewd dodge among the cravens of taking six or eight able bodied soldiers to assist some slightly wounded fellow into the hospital; and between this cordon and the rear of the fighting divisions the fragments of regiments were reorganized after a fashion, and sent back to the field. Brigades could not be got together again, much less divisions, but the regiments pieced together from the loose squads that could be gathered and officered, often by men who could find scarcely a soldier of their own commands, were hurried to the front, and many of them did good service.

    It was fortunate for us that the accidental circumstance that Prentiss' portion of our line had been completely broken sooner than any of the rest, had caused the enemy's onset to veer chiefly to our left. There we were tolerably safe; and at worst, if the rebels drove us to the river on the left bank, the gunboats could come into play. Our weakest point was the right, and to turning this the rebels do not seem to have paid so much attention on Sunday. According to general understanding, in the event of an attack at Pittsburg Landing, Major General Lew Wallace was to come in on our right and flank the rebels by marching across from Crump's Landing below.

Yet strangely enough, Wallace, though with his division all drawn up and ready to march anywhere at a moment's notice, was not ordered to Pittsburg Landing till nearly if not quite twelve o'clock. Then, through misdirection as to the way to get on the new road, four miles of marching were lost, and its circuitous route made it twelve miles more before they could reach the scene of battle. Meantime, our right was almost wholly unprotected.

Fortunately, as I said, however, the rebels do not seem to have discovered the full extent of this weakness, and their heaviest fighting was done on the center and left, where we still preserved our line.

Hurlburt's Division

Hurlburt's division, it will be remembered, stretched across the Corinth road, facing rather to our left. W. H. L. Wallace's other brigades had gone over to assist McArthur, and the division, thus reunited, steadily closed the line, where Prentiss' division and Stuart's brigade, in their retreat, had left it open. To Hurlburt's right the lines were patched out with the reorganized regiments that had been resent to the field. McClernand and Sherman were both there.

Hurlburt had been encamped in the edge nearest the river of a stretch of open fields, backed with heavy timber. Among his troops were the Seventeenth and Twenty-fifth Kentucky, Forty-fourth and Thirty-first

Indiana, constituting Lauman's brigade: Third Iowa, Forty-first Illinois and some others, forming Colonel

Williams' Brigade

As Prentiss fell back Hurlburt's left aided Wallace in sustaining the rebel onset, and when McClernand gave way the remainder of the division was thrown forward. The position beyond the camps, however, was not a good one, and the division was compelled to fall back through its camp to the thick woods behind. Here, with open fields before them, they could rake the rebel approach. Nobly did they now stand their ground. From ten to half-past three they held the enemy in check, and through nearly that whole time were actively engaged. Hurlburt himself displayed the most daring and brilliant gallantry, and his example, with that of the brave officers under him, nerved the men to the sternest endurance.

Three times during those long hours the heavy rebel masses on the left charged upon the division, and three times were they repulsed with terrible slaughter. Close, sharp, continuous musketry, whole lines belching fire on the rebels as the leaden storm swept the fields over which they attempted to advance, were too much for rebel discipline, though the bodies left scattered over the fields, even on Monday evening, bore ghastly testimony to the daring with which they had been precipitated towards our lines.

But there is still much in the Napoleonic theory that Providence has a tendency at least to go with the heaviest battalions. The battalions were against us. The rebel generals, too, handled their forces with a skill that extorted admiration in the midst of our sufferings. Repulse was nothing to them; if a rush on our lines failed, they took their disordered troops to the rear, and sent up fresh troops, who, unknowing the fearful reception awaiting them, were ready to try it again. The jaded division was compelled to yield, and after six hours' magnificent fighting, it fell back out of sight of its camps, and to a point within half a mile of the landing.

Wallace's Brigade – The Leader Wounded

Let us turn to the fate of Hurlburt's companion division—that of Brigadier General W. H. L. Wallace, which included the Second and Seventh Iowa, Ninth and Twenty-eighth Illinois, and several of the other regiments composing Major General Smith's old division. Wallace had also three excellent batteries Stone's, Richardson's, and Weber's (all from Missouri) formerly an artillery battalion, under the general management of Major Cavender.

With him, too, the fight began about ten o'clock, as already described. From that time till four in the afternoon they manfully bore up. The musketry fire was absolutely continuous; there was scarcely a moment that some part of the line was not pouring in their rattling volleys, and the artillery was admirably served, with but little intermission through the entire time.

Once or twice the infantry advanced, attempting to drive the continually increasing enemy; but though they could hold what they had, their numbers were not equal to the tank of conquering any more.

Four separate times in turn the rebels attempted to charge on them. Each time the infantry poured in its quickest volleys, the artillery redoubled its exertions, and the rebels retreated with heavy slaughter. The division was eager to remain, even when Hurlburt fell back, and the fine fellows with the guns were particularly indignant at not being permitted to pound away. But their supports were gone on either side; to have remained in isolated advance would have been madness. Just as the necessity for retreating was becoming apparent General Wallace, whose cool, collected bravery had commanded the admiration or all, was, as it was thought, mortally wounded, and was borne away from the field. At last the division fell back. Its soldiers claim—justly I believe the proud distinction of being the last to yield in the general break of our lines that gloomy Sunday afternoon, which, at half-past four o'clock, had left most of our army within half a mile of the Landing, with the rebels up to a thousand yards of their position.

Captain Stone could not resist the temptation of stopping, as he passed what had been Hurlburt's headquarters, to try a few parting shots. He did fine execution, but narrowly escaped losing some guns by having his wheel horses shot down. Captain Walker did lose a twenty-pounder through some breakage in the carriage. It was recovered again on Monday.

The Close of Sunday's Fight

We have reached the last act in the tragedy of Sunday. It is half past four o'clock. Our front line of divisions has been lost since half-past ten. Our reserve line is now gone, too. The rebels occupy the camps of every division save that of W. H. L. Wallace. Our whole army is crowded in the region of Wallace's camps and to a circuit of half to two-thirds of a mile around the landing. We have been falling back all day. We can do it no more. The next repulse puts us into the river, and there are not transports enough to cross a single division till the enemy would be upon us.

Lew Wallace's division might turn the tide for us—it is made of fighting men—but where is it? Why has it not been thundering on the right for three hours past? We do not know yet that it was not ordered up until noon. Buell is coming, but he has been doing it all day, and all last week. His advance guard is across the river now, waiting ferriage; but what is an advance guard against sixty-thousand victorious foes in front of us.

We have lost nearly all our camps and camp equipage. We have lost nearly half our field artillery. We have lost a division general and two or three regiments of soldiers as prisoners. We have lost—how dreadfully we are to think—in killed and wounded. The hospitals are full to overflowing. A long ridge bluff is set aside for surgical uses. It is covered with the maimed, the dead and dying. And our men are discouraged by prolonged defeat. Nothing but the most energetic exertions on the officers prevents them from becoming demoralized. Regiments have lost their favorite field officers, companies the captains they have always looked to, with that implicit faith that soldiers learn, to lead them to battle.

Meantime there is a lull in the fighting. For the first time since sunrise you fail to catch the angry rattle of musketry or the heavy booming of the field guns. Either the enemy must be preparing for the grand final rush that is to crown the day's success and save the Southern Confederacy, or they are puzzled by our last retreat, and are moving cautiously, lest we spring some trap upon them. Let us embrace the opportunity and look about the landing. We pass the old log house, lately Post Office, now full of wounded and surgeons; which constitutes the "Pittsburg" part of the landing. General Grant and staff are in a group beside it. The general is confident. "We can hold them off till tomorrow, then they'll be exhausted, and we can go at them with fresh troops." A great crowd is collected around the building, all in uniforms, most of them with guns. And yet we are needing troops in front so sorely!

Cowards

On the bluffs above the river there is a sight that may well make our cheeks tingle with shame for some of our soldiers. There are not less than three thousand skulkers lining the banks. Ask them why they don't go to their places in the line: "Oh, our regiment is all cut to piece." "Why don't you go to where it is forming again?" "I can't find It," and the sulk look as if that would be the very last thing he would want to do.

Officers are around among them, trying to hunt up their men, storming, coaxing, commanding—cursing I am afraid. One strange fellow—a major, if I remember aright—is making a sort of elevated, superfine Fourth of July speech to everybody that will listen to him. He means well, certainly: "Men of Kentucky, of Illinois, of Ohio, of Iowa, of Indiana, I Implore you, I beg of you. Come up now. Help us through two hours more. By all that you hold dear, by the homes you hope to defend, by the flag you love, by the States you honor, by all your love of country, by all your hatred of treason. I conjure you, come up and do your duty now." And so on for quantity "That feller's a good speaker," was the only response I heard, and the fellow who gave it nestled more snugly behind his tree as he spoke.

I knew well enough the nature of the skulking animal in an army during a battle. I had seen their performances before, but never on so large a scale never with such an utter sickness of heart as I looked, as now. Still. I do not believe there was very much more than the average per centage. It was a big army, and the runaways all sought the landing.

Arrival of General Buell

Looking across the Tennessee we see a body of cavalry, awaiting transportation over. They are said to be Buell's advance, yet they have been there an hour or two alone. But suddenly there is a rustle among the runaways. It is, it is! You see the gleaming of the gun barrels, you catch among the leaves and undergrowth down the opposite side of the river glimpses of the steady, swinging tramp of trained soldiers. A division of Buell's army is here! And the men who have left their regiments on the field send up three cheers for Buell. They cheering! May it parch their throats, as if they had been breathing the simoon.

Here comes a boat across with a Lieutenant and two or three privates of the Signal Corps. Some orders are instantly given the officer, and as instantly telegraphed to the other side by the mysterious waving and raising and dropping of the flags, A steamer comes up with pontoons on board, with which a bridge could be speedily thrown across. Unaccountably enough, to onlookers, she slowly reconnoiters and steams back again. Perhaps, after all, it is better to have no bridge there. It simplifies the questions, takes escape out of the count, and leaves it to victory or death—to the cowards that slink behind the bluffs as well as to the brave men who peril their lives to do the State some service on the fields beyond. Preparations go rapidly forward for crossing the division (General Nelson's which has the advance of Buell's army) on the dozen or so transports that have been tied up along the bank.

We have spent but a few minutes on the bluff, but they are the golden minutes that count for years. Well was it for that driven, defeated, but not disgraced army of General Grant's, that those minutes were improved. Colonel Webster, the chief of staff, and an artillery officer of no mean ability had arranged the guns that he could collect, of those that remained to us, in a sort of semicircle, protecting the Landing, and bearing chiefly on our center and left by which the rebels were pretty sure to advance. Corps of artillerists to man them were improvised from all the batteries that could be collected. Twenty-two guns in all were placed in position. Two of them were very heavy siege guns, long thirty-twos. Where they came from I do not know, what battery they belonged to I have no idea; I only know that they were there, in the right place, half a mile back from the bluff, sweeping the approaches by the left, and by the ridge Corinth road; that there was nobody to work them; that Dr. Cornyn, surgeon of Frank Blair's First Missouri Artillery, proffered his services that they were gladly accepted, and that he did work them to such effect as to lay out ample work for scores of his professional brethren on the other side of the fight.

Remember the situation. It was half-past four o'clock? perhaps a quarter later still. Every division of our army on the field had been repulsed. The enemy were in the camps of four out of five of them. We were driven to within little over half a mile of the Landing. Behind us was a deep, rapid river. Before us was a victorious enemy. And still there was an hour for fighting. "Oh, that night or Blucher would come!" Oh, that night or Lew Wallace would come! Nelson's division of Buell's army evidently couldn't cross in time to do us much good. We didn't yet know why Lew Wallace wasn't on the ground. In the justice of a righteous cause, and in that semi-circle of twenty-two guns in position, lay all the hope we could see.

Suddenly a broad, sulfurous flash of light leaped out from the darkening woods, and through the glare and smoke came whistling the leaden hail. The rebels were making their crowning effort for the day, and as was expected when our guns were hastily placed, they came from our left and center. They had wasted their fire at 1,000 yards. Instantaneously our deep-mouthed bulldogs flung out their sonorous response. The rebel artillery opened, and shell and round shot came tearing across the open space back of the bluff. May I be forgiven for the malicious thought, but I certainly did wish one or two might drop behind the bluff among the crowd of skulkers hovering under the hill at the river's edge.

Very handsome was the response our broken infantry battalions poured in. The enemy soon had reason to remember that, if not still in their ashes live the wonted fires, at least still in the fragments lived the ancient valor that had made the short-lived rebel successes already cost so dear.

The Gunboats Open Fire

The rebel infantry gained no ground, but the furious cannonading and musketry continued. Suddenly new actors entered on the stage. Our Cincinnati wooden gunboats, the A. O. Taylor, and the Lexington, had been all day impatiently chafing for their time to come. The opportunity was theirs. The rebels were attacking on our left, lying where Stuart's brigade had lain on Licking Creek in the morning, and stretching thence in on the Hamburg road, and across toward our old center as far as Hurlburt's camps. Steaming up to the mouth of the little creek the boats rounded to. There was the ravine, cut through the bluff as if on purpose for their shells.

Eager to avenge the death of their commanding General (now known to have been killed a couple of hours before), and to complete the victory they believed to be within their grasp, the rebels had incautiously ventured within reach of their most dreaded antagonists, as broadside after broadside of seven-inch shells and sixty-four pound shot soon taught them. This was a foe they had hardly counted on, and the unexpected fire in flank and rear sadly disconcerted their well laid plans. The boats fired admirably, and with a rapidity that was astonishing. Our twenty-two land guns kept up their stormy thunder: and thus, amid a crash and roar, and scream of shells and demon-like hiss of Minnie balls, that Sabbath evening wore away We held the enemy at bay; it was enough. The prospect for the morrow was foreboding; but sufficient unto the day is the evil thereof. We had had plenty of evil that day—of course, therefore, the text was applicable. Before dark the Thirty-sixth Indiana, from Nelson's advance brigade, had crossed, advanced into line with Grant's forces at the double quick and had put in fourteen rounds as an earnest of what should be forthcoming on the morrow.

The enemy suddenly slackened his fire. His grand object had been defeated; he had not finished his task in a day: but there is evidence that officers and men alike shared the confidence that their morning assault would be final.

As the sounds of battle died away, and division generals drew off their men, Buell had arrived, and Lew Wallace had been heard from. Both would be ready by morning, and council of war was held, and it was decided that as soon as possible after daybreak we should attack the enemy, now snugly quartered in our camps. Lew Wallace, who was coming in on the new road from Crump's Landing and crossing Snake Creek just above the Illinois Wallace's (W. H. L.) camps, was to take the right and sweep back toward the position from which Sherman had been driven on Sunday morning. Nelson was to take the extreme left. Buell promised to put in

Tom Crittenden next to Nelson, and McCook next to him by a seasonable hour in the morning. The gap between McCook and Lew Wallace was to be filled with the reorganized
division of Grant's old army; Hurlburt coming next to McCook, then McClernand, and Sherman closing the gap between McClernand and Lew Wallace.

The Night Between Two Battles

Stealthily the troops crept to their new positions and lay down in line of battle on their arms. All through the night Buell's men were marching up from Savannah to the point opposite Pittsburg Landing, and being ferried across, or were coming up on transports. By an hour after dark Wallace had his division in. Through the misdirection he had received, he had started on the Snake Creek road proper, which would have brought him in on the enemy's rear, miles from support, and where he would have been gobbled at a mouthful. Getting back to the right road had delayed him. He at once ascertained the position of certain rebel batteries which lay in front of him on our right, that threatened absolutely to bar his advance in the morning, and selected positions for a couple of his batteries from which they could silence the one he dreaded. Placing these in position, and arranging his brigade for support, took him till one o'clock in the morning. Then his wearied men lay down to snatch a few hours of sleep before entering into the valley of the Shadow of Death on the morrow.

By nine o'clock all was hushed near the landing. The host of combatants that three hours before had been deep in the work of human destruction had all sunk silently to earth, the wearied to sleep, the wounded to die." The stars looked out upon the scene, and all breathed the natural quiet and calm of a Sabbath evening. But presently there came a flash that spread like sheet lightning over the ripples of the river current, and the roar of a heavy naval gun went echoing up and down the bluffs, through the unusual stillness of the night. Others speedily followed. By the flash you could just discern the black outline of the piratical looking hull, and see how the gunboat gracefully settled into the water at the recoil; the smoke soon cast up a thin vail that seemed only to soften and sweeten the scene; from the woods away inland you caught faintly the muffled explosion of the shell, like the knell of the spirit that was taking its flight.

We knew nothing then of the effect of this gunboat cannonading, which was vigorously kept up till nearly morning, and it only served to remind us the more vividly of the day's disasters, of the fact that half a mile off lay a victorious enemy, commanded by the most dashing of their Generals, and of the question one scarcely dared ask himself, "What tomorrow?" We were defeated, our dead and dying were around us, days could hardly sum up our losses. And then there came up the grand refrain of Whittier—written after Manassas, I believe, but on that night apparently far more applicable to this greater than Manassas. "Under the Cloud and Through the Sea."

Sons of the saints who faced their Jordan flood,
In fierce Atlantic's un-retreating wave.
Who by the Red Sea of their glorious blood
Reached to the Freedom that you blood shall save!

0 countrymen! God's day is not yet done!
He leaveth not his people utterly!
Count it a covenant, that he leads us on
Beneath the cloud and through the crlmon sea!

The Battle on Monday

The Work of Sunday Night

With the exception of the gunboat bombardment, the night seemed to have passed in entire quiet. A heavy thunder storm had come up about midnight, and, though we were all shivering over the ducking, the surgeons assured us that a better thing could not have happened. The ground, they said, was covered with wounded not yet found, or whom we were unable to bring from the field. The moisture would to some extent cool the burning, parching thirst, which is one of the chief terrors of lying wounded and helpless on the battle field, and the falling water was the best dressing for the wounds.

The regiments of Buell's divisions were still disembarking at the Landing. Many had taken their places; the rest hurried on out as fast as they landed and fell in to the rear of their brigade line, for reserves. I stood for a few moments at the Landing, curious to see how these few fellows would march out to the field where they knew reverses had crowded so thickly upon us the day before, and where many of them must lie down to sleep his last sleep ere the sun, then rising, should sink again. There was little of that vulgar vanity of valor which was so conspicuous in all the movements or our rawer troops eight or nine months ago. There was no noisy and senseless yelling, no shouting of boasts, no calling onlookers on to "show us where the cowardly seccesh is and we'll clean 'em out double quick." These men understood the work before them. They went to it as brave men should, determinedly, hopefully, calmly.

It soon becoming evident that the gunboat bombardment through the night had not been without a most important effect in changing the very conditions under which we renewed the struggle. The sun had gone down with the enemy's lines clasping us tight on the center and left, pushing us to the river, and leaving as little over half a mile out into all the broad space we had held in the morning. The gunboats had cut the coils and loosened the constriction. As we soon learned, their shells had made the old position of our extreme left, which the rebels had been pleasantly occupying, utterly untenable instead of being able to slip up on us through the night as they had probably intended, they were compelled to fall back from point to point; each time as they had found places they thought out of range, a shell would come dropping in; nowhere within range could they lie but the troublesome visitors would find them out, and to end the matter they fell back beyond our inner camps, and thus lost more than half the ground they had gained by our four o'clock retreat the afternoon before.

Less easily accounted for was a movement of theirs on our right. They had held here a steep bluff, covered with underbrush, as their advanced line. Through the night they abandoned this, which gave them the best possible position for opposing Lew Wallace and had fallen back across some open fields to the scrub oak woods beyond. The advantage of compelling our advance over unprotected openings, while they maintained a sheltered position, was obvious, but certainly not so great as that of holding a height which artillery and infantry would make as difficult to take as many a fort. Nevertheless, they fell back.

Want of System on Our Side

The reader who is patient enough to wade through this narration will scarcely fail to observe that thus far I have said little or nothing of any plan of attack or defense among our commanders. It has been, simply, because I have failed to see any evidence of such a plan. To me it seemed on Sunday as if every division general at least—not to say in many cases, every individual soldier—imitated the good old Israelitish plan of action, by which every man did what seemed good in his own eyes. There may have been an infinite amount of generalship displayed, in superintending our various defeats and reformations and retreats, but to me it seemed of that microscopic character that required the magnifying powers of a special permit for exclusive newspaper telegraphing on government lines to discover.

Sunday night there was, as has been said, a council of war, but if the Major General commanding developed any plans there beyond the simple arrangement of our line of battle. I am very certain that some of the division commanders didn't find it out. Stubborn fighting alone delayed our losses on Sunday; stubborn fighting alone saved us when we had reached the point beyond which came the child's "jumping off place:" and stubborn fighting, with such generalship as individual division commanders displayed, regained on Monday what we had lost before.

To those who had looked despairingly at the prospects Sunday evening, it seemed strange that the rebels did not open out on us by daybreak again. Their retreat before the bombshells of the gunboats, however, explained the delay. Our own divisions were put in motion almost simultaneously. By seven o'clock Lew Wallace opened the ball by shelling, from the positions he had selected the night before, the rebel battery, of which mention has been made—a brisk artillery duel, a rapid movement of infantry across a shallow ravine as if to storm, and the rebels, enfiladed and menaced in front, limbered up and made the opening of their Monday's retreating.

Nelson's Advance

To the left we were slower in finding the enemy. They had been compelled to travel some distance to get out of gunboat's range. Nelson moved his division about the same time Wallace opened on the rebel battery, forming in line of battle, Ammon's brigade on the extreme left, Bruce's in the center, and Hazen's to the right. Skirmishers were thrown out, and for nearly or quite a mile the division thus swept the country, pushing a few outlying rebels before it, till it came upon them in force. Then a general engagement broke out along the line, and again the rattle of musketry and thunder of artillery echoed over the late silent fields. There was no straggling this morning. Those men were better drilled than many of those whose regiments had broken to pieces on the day before, and strict measures were taken, at any rate, to prevent the miscellaneous thronging back out of harm's way. They stood up to their work and did their duty manfully.

It soon became evident that, whether from change of commanders or some other cause, the rebels were pursuing a different policy in massing their forces. On Sunday the heaviest fighting had been done on the left. This morning they seemed to make less determined resistance here, while toward the center and right the ground was more obstinately contested, and the struggle longer prolonged.

Until half pest ten o'clock Nelson advanced slowly but steadily, sweeping his long lines over the ground of our core defeat on Sunday morning, forward over scores of dead rebels, resistlessly pressing back the jaded and wearied enemy. The rebels had received but few reinforcements during the night, their men were exhausted with their desperate contest of the day before, and manifestly dispirited by the evident fact that, notwithstanding their well laid plans of destruction in detail, they were fighting Grant and Buell combined.

Gradually, as Nelson pushed forward his lines under heavy musketry the enemy fall back, till about half-past ten, when, under cover of the heavy timber and a furious cannonading, they made a general rally. Our forces, flushed with their easy victory, were scarcely prepared for the sudden onset where retreat had been all they had been seeing before. Suddenly the rebel masses were hurled against our lines with tremendous force. Our men halted, wavered and fell back. At this critical juncture Captain Terry's regular battery came dashing up. Scarcely taking time to unlimber he was loading and sighting his pieces before the caissons had turned, and in an instant was tossing in shell from twenty-four-pound howitzers to the compact and advancing rebel ranks.

Here was the turning point of the battle on the left. The rebels were only checked, not halted. On they came. Horse after horse from the batteries was picked off. Every private at one of the howitzers fell, and the gun was worked by Captain Terry himself and a corporal. The rebels seemed advancing. A regiment dashed up from our line and saved the disabled piece. Then for two hours artillery and musketry at close range. At last they began to waver. Our men pressed on, pouring in deadly volleys. Just then Buell, who assumed the general direction of his troops in the field, came up. At a glance he saw the chance. "Forward at double quick by brigades." Our men leaped forward as if they had been tied and were only too much rejoiced to be able to move. For a quarter of a mile the rebels fell back. Faster and faster they ran. Less and less resistance was made to the advance. At last the front camps on the left were reached, and by half past two that point was cleared. The rebels had been steadily swept back over the ground they had won with heavy losses, as they fell into confusion, we had retaken all our own guns lost here the day before, and one or two from the rebels were left as trophies to tell in after days how bravely that great victory over treason in Tennessee was won.

Advance of Crittenden's Division

I have sketched the advance of Nelson. Next to him came Crittenden. He too swept forward over his ground to the front some distance before finding the foe. Between eight and nine o'clock, however, while keeping Smith's brigade on his left up even with Nelson's flank, in the grand advance, they came upon the enemy with a battery in position, and, well supported, Smith dashed his brigade forward: there was sharp, close work with musketry and the rebels fled. We had three pieces—a twelve-pound howitzer and two brass six pounders. But they cost the gallant Sixteenth Ohio dear. Major Ben Platt Runkle fell, mortally wounded. Softly may he sleep, and green grow the laurels over his honored grave. None worthier wear them living.

For half an hour, perhaps, the storm raged around these captured guns Then came the reflex rebel wave that had hurled Nelson back. Crittenden, too, caught its full force. The rebels swept up to the batteries around them, and on down after our retreating column. But the two brigades, like those of Nelson to the left, took a fresh position, faced the foe, and held their ground. Mendenhall's and Bartlett's batteries now began shelling the infantry that alone opposed them. Before abandoning the guns so briefly held, they had spiked them with mud, and the novel expedient was perfectly successful. From that time till after one o'clock, while the fight raged back and forth over the same ground, the rebels did not succeed in firing a shot from their mud-spiked artillery.

At last our brigades began to gain the advantage again. Crittenden pushed them steadily forward Mendenhall, with his accomplished First Lieutenant Parsons, one of our Western Reserve West Pointers, and Bartlett, poured in their shell. A rush for the contested battery and it is ours again. The rebels retreated towards the left. Smith and Boyle holding the infantry well in hand, Mendenhall again got their range and poured in shell on the new position. The fortune of the day was against them, as against their comrades to Nelson's front, and they were soon in full retreat.

Just then Brigadier General Thomas J. Woods' advance brigade from his approaching division came up. It was too late for the fight, but it relieved Crittenden's weary fellows, and pushed on after the rebels until they were found to have left our most advanced camps.

McCook's Advance

Thus, the left was saved. Meanwhile McCook, with as magnificent a regiment as ever came from the army of the Potomac, or from any army of volunteers in the world, was doing equally well toward the center. His division was handled in such a way as to save great effusion of blood, while equally important results were attained. Thus, the reserves were kept as much as possible from under fire, while those to the front were engaged. Thus, the lists of killed and wounded will show that while as heavy fighting was done here as anywhere on the right or center, the casualties are fewer than could have been expected.

It would scarcely be interesting to prolong details where the course of one division so nearly resembled that of the others. But let me sketch the close. An Illinois battery, serving in the division, was in imminent danger. The Sixth Indiana was ordered to its relief. A rapid rush, close musketry—firing no need of bayonets here—the battery is safe. The enemy are to the front and right. Advancing and firing right oblique the Sixth pushes on. The rebel colors fall. Another volley; they fall again. Another volley; yet once more the fated colors drop. There is fatality in it; so, the rebels seem to think at least, as they wheel and disappear.

And then Rosseau's brigade is drawn off, in splendid style as if coming in from parade, conscious of some grand master of reviews watching their movements. So, there was—the rebel General. As he saw the brigade filing back, he pushed his forces forward again. Kirk's brigade advanced to meet them coming out of the woods into an open field to do so. They were met by a tremendous fire which threw a battalion of regulars in front of them (under Major Oliver, I think) into some confusion. They retire to reform, and meanwhile down drops the brigade flat on the ground. Then, as the front is clear, they spring up, charge across the open field—never mind the falling straight on, on to the woods, under cover, with the enemy driven back by the impetuous advance. And now he rallies. Fierce musketry firing sweeps the woods. They advance thirty rods, perhaps when the Twenty-ninth Indiana gets into a marsh and falls partially to the rear. Heavier comes the leaden hail. Twenty-ninth and Thirtieth both fall back fifteen or twenty rods; they rally and advance, again they are hurled back; again, they start forward, and this time they come in on the vulnerable points. The enemy flees. Colonel Waggoner's Fifteenth Indiana comes up to the support, the enemy disappear, fresh troops take their places, and for them the fight is ended. I might describe similar deeds of Willich's and Harrison's regiments, but, "from one, learn all."

McClernand and Hurlburt

Farther to the right McClernand and Hurlburt were gallantly coming on with their jaded men. The soldiers would fight—that was the great lesson of the battle. If surprised and driven off in consequence of surprise, that can hardly be wholly charged on them. Four times McClernand regained and lost again the ground to the front of his division. Similar were Hurlburt's fortunes.

But I must abandon these details. Beginning at the left we have followed the wave of successes that swept us forward again, from spot to spot, over the hard-lost fields of Sunday, our paeans of victory the wild cheers of our successful soldiers sounding the requiem of the fallen rebels, who have atoned for their treason by the brave man's death. Nelson, Crittenden, McCook, Hurlburt, McClernand have borne their divisions through the fray. It lasted longer on the right and was as rarely interesting as the chess game of a master. Let's trace it through.

Lew Wallace's Movements

In speaking of the opening of Monday's battle, I mentioned Major General Lew Wallace's opening the ball at seven o'clock, by shelling with enfilading fires a rebel battery. A few shots demonstrated to the rebels that their position was untenable. The instant Sherman came in to protect his left, Wallace advanced his infantry. The rebel battery at once limbered up and got out of the way. The advance had withdrawn the division from Sherman, making a left half wheel, to get back into the neighborhood of our line; they advanced some two hundred yards, which brought them to a little elevation, with a broad open stretch to the front. As the division halted on the crest of the swell, there passed before them a rare vision. Away to the front were woods. Through the edge of the timber, skirting the fields the head of a rebel column appeared, marching past in splendid style on the double quick. Banner after banner appeared; the "Stars and Bars," formed a long line, stretching parallel with Wallace's line of battle. Regiment after regiment appeared, the line lengthened, and doubled and trebled; the head of the column was out of sight and still they came. Twenty regiments were counted passing through the woods. The design was plain. The rebels had abandoned the idea of forcing their way through our left, and now the manifest attempt was to turn our right.

Batteries were now ordered up—Thompson's and Thurber's—and the whole column was shelled as it passed. The rebels rapidly threw their artillery into position. and a brisk cannonading began. After a time, while the fight still rested with the artillery, the rebels opened a new and destructive battery to the right, which our men soon learned to know as "Watson's Louisiana Battery," from the marks on the ammunition boxes they forced it from time to time to leave behind.

Batteries, with a brigade of supporting infantry, were now moved forward over open field, under heavy fire, to contend against this new assailant. The batteries opened, the sharpshooters were thrown out to the front to pick off the rebel artillerists, the brigade was ordered down on its face to protect it from the flying shell and grape. For an hour and a half, the contest lasted, while the body of the division was still delayed, waiting for Sherman. By ten o'clock Sherman's right, under Colonel Marsh, came up. He started to move across the fields. The storm of musketry and grape was too much for him, and he fell back in good order. Again, he started on the double and gained the woods. The Louisiana battery was turned; Marsh's position left it subject to fire in flank in front, and then fled. The other rebel batteries at once did the same, and Wallace's division, up in an instant, now that a master move had swept the board, pushed forward. Before them were broad fallow fields, then a woody little ravine, then corn fields, then woods.

The left brigade was sent forward. It crossed the fallow fields, under ordinary fire, then gained the ravine, and was rushing across the cornfields, when the same Louisiana steel rifled guns opened on them. Dashing forward they reached a little ground swell, behind which they dropped like dead men; while skirmishers were sent forward to silence the troublesome battery. The skirmishers crawled forward till they gained a little knell, not more than seventy-five yards from the battery. Of course, the battery opened on them. They replied, if not so noisy, more to the purpose. In a few minutes the battery was driven off, with artillerists killed, horses shot down, and badly crippled every way. But the affair cost us a brave man—Lieutenant Colonel Garber—who could not control his enthusiasm at the conduct of the skirmishers, and in his excitement incautiously exposed himself. All this while rebel regiments were pouring up to attack the audacious brigade that was supporting the skirmishers, and fresh regiments from Wallace's division came up in time to checkmate the game.

But the battery was silenced. "Forward" was the division order. Rushing across the cornfields under heavy fire, they now met the rebels face to face in the woods.

The contest was quick, decisive. Close, sharp, continuous musketry for a few minutes, and the rebels fell back.

Here unfortunately, Sherman's right gave way. Wallace's flank was exposed. He instantly formed Colonel Wood's (Seventy-sixth Ohio) in a new line of battle, in right angles with the real one, and with orders to protect the flank. The Eleventh Indiana was likewise here in a sharp engagement with the enemy attempting to flank, and for a time the contest waxed fierce. But Sherman soon filled the place of his broken regiments, again Wallace's division poured forward, and again the enemy gave way.

By two o'clock the division was into the woods again, and for three-quarters of a mile it advanced under a continuous storm of shot. Then another contest or two with batteries, always met with skirmishers and sharpshooting—then, by four o'clock, two hours later than on the right, a general rebel retreat—then pursuit, recall and encampment on the old grounds of Sherman's division, in the very tents from which those regiments were driven that hapless Sunday morning.

The camps were regained, the rebels were repulsed, their attack had failed; we stood where we began rebel cavalry were within half a mile of us; the retreating columns were within striking distance. But we had regained our camps. And so, ended the battle of Pittsburg.

The Killed and Wounded

I do not pretend to give more than an estimate, but I have made the estimate with some care, going to the Adjutants of different regiments that had been in as heavy fighting as any, getting statements of their losses—sure to be very nearly, if not quite, accurate and approximating thus from the loss of a dozen regiments to the probable loss of all. I have ridden over the grounds, too—have seen the dead and wounded lying over the field—have noted the number in the hospitals end on the boats. As the result of it all, I do not believe our loss in killed and wounded will number over thirty-five hundred to four-thousand. The question of prisoners is another matter.

Reports that certain regiments only have half the men answering roll call indicate nothing. The regiments are all more or less disorganized and the soldiers scattered everywhere. Many go home with the sick, many are nurses in the hospitals, many keep out of sight seeing all they can.

The Guthrie Gray regiment lost very slightly. No commissioned officer received any wound even, except Lieutenant Colonel Anderson; and his is only from a spent ball.

In the Forty-eighth Ohio, Colonel Sullivan was slightly wounded; Captain Warner, killed; Lieutenant Plyley, severely wounded; Captain Bond, severely; Lieutenant Lindsay, slightly; Lieutenant Pusegate, slightly. These are all the casualties among the commissioned officers of the regiment.

The Numbers Engaged

The best opinions of the strength with which the rebels attacked us place their numbers at sixty-thousand. They may have been reinforced five to ten-thousand Sunday night.

Grant had scarcely forty-thousand effective men on Sunday. Of these, half a dozen regiments were utterly raw—had scarcely had their guns long enough to know how to handle them. Some were supplied with weapons on their way up.

Buell had three divisions that took part in the action Nelson's, Crittenden's and McCook's. They numbered say twenty-thousand—a liberal estimate. Lew Wallace came up on Monday with say eleven-thousand more. That gives us, counting the Sunday men as all effective again, sixty-seven thousand on Monday, on our side, against sixty to seventy thousand rebels. It was not numbers that gained us the day. It was fighting. All honor to our Northern soldiers for it.

Account of James R. Scott

*(This letter was originally published in the **Wood County Reporter** (Wisconsin), April 19, 1862. It is from Private James R. Scott to his wife and gives a soldier's eye view of the battle on both days.)*

Pittsburg Landing, Tenn.,
April 10, 1862.

Dear Wife: —We arrived here last Saturday night and immediately proceeded to camp, distant about four miles. Pitched our tents, with a short allowance of provisions, for the night.

While eating breakfast on Sunday morning, the long roll sounded to fall into battle line, and in less than half an hour the enemy were upon us, advancing through the bushes, conveying the Union Colors. Word was given our Colonel that they were a regiment of our pickets retreating. When getting within eighty feet of us they opened fire, which we returned laying upon the ground loading and firing 'till they drove us across an open field of about forty acres, when we again rallied and delivered our fire from behind the trees.

We were again driven back 'till we came to the second line which had just formed. Then our men rested for about half an hour when we again formed and advanced. In this advance, about eleven o'clock our Colonel was wounded and has since died. The Lieut. Colonel was badly wounded. Our Major was killed, as was also our acting adjutant, shot through the head leaving us without a field officer. What was left of the regiment stood another charge, in which Capt. Compton was killed. Our colors, and the Color Bearer, John Snyder, we cannot find. He is probably a prisoner. We have suffered terribly. Out of ten captains, eight of whom were in the engagement, but two are left. The Lieutenants suffered badly, but I think many were captured.

I never heard hail stones fall thicker and faster than did the bullets around us. Joseph Bullock was shot in the breast [during] the first fire. He was helped into a tent, but we have not seen him since, nor have we found his body. He is probably captured. Mr. Eaton, Grundy's father-in-law and Andrew Loomis, were also wounded. They fell back to the river and got on board the boats. McRaith has not been heard from since Sunday morning; but he may yet come in, as prisoners are constantly escaping from the enemy and returning.

We were driven within one mile of the Landing, when the gunboats came to our assistance, and the advance of Gen. Buell's reinforcements (15,000 strong) appeared in sight. They had marched twelve miles on a double-quick, and giving three cheers they charged upon the enemy, who, after fighting three hours, fell back three-quarters of a mile.

Our troops slept on their arms during the night of Sunday, in a drenching rain, without tents or victuals. Early on Monday morning the battle commenced anew and raged without cessation till about five o'clock in the afternoon. Thunder, the loudest you ever heard, was no comparison to the roar of artillery and small arms which was kept up till the enemy ran.

It is the opinion here that this is the last large battle. Beauregard, Bragg, and Johnson, with their united forces, were here and fought desperately to gain the day. On Sunday they outnumbered us four to one. On Sunday night, we had reinforcements to the extent of 70,000 men and 80 cannon which gave us on Monday a decided victory. Troops have been rushing in ever since and following up the enemy.

They may make a stand at Corinth, twenty miles from here, but our Generals think they will not be able to reorganize the army so as to accomplish much, as Gen. Buell has been pursuing them from the commencement of the retreat. Since the fight we have been collecting the wounded and burying the dead and are not through yet. The field was the most horrible sight I ever saw. In one field it was almost impossible to step without treading on the dead and wounded. In a number of places, I saw them in piles from four to ten deep.

Account of Sgt. H. M. White

*(Following is a letter from Sergeant H. M. White to his friend C. Elliott of West Liberty, Iowa. It was printed in **The Muscatine Weekly Journal** (Iowa). May 2, 1862. Again, it is a good look at the regular soldier in the fighting. At the end, he betrays his distrust of General Grant, and how glad his regiment was when General Don Carlos Buell took the field.)*

FRIEND:
I dare say you are at this moment better posted in regard to the "great battle of Pittsburg Landing" than your humble servant, who had the good fortune to be here at and during the fight. Nevertheless, I am certain you will not be content until you receive a full, true and particular account from your own correspondent—so here goes.

In the first place, endeavor to fix in your mind the location of a few prominent points.

Pittsburg Landing (a simple landing place, with no houses) stands on the west bank of the Tennessee river, some ten miles south of Savannah. From the Landing, a road leaves the river, and, running at an angle of some 45° from the river for the distance of three miles, reaches the camping ground of our brigade (the 8th and 18th

Illinois, and the 11th and 13th Iowa). Thus, you see, we are at the southwest of Pittsburg, while, some twenty miles to the southwest of us, lies Corinth, the crossing of the Memphis and Charleston, and Mobile and Ohio railroads. South of us, and between here and Corinth, is an extensive swamp which, starting from the river, extends several miles to the west. Through this swamp, with a view of transporting our heavy artillery and baggage, our Generals had constructed a causeway, but, unfortunately, we never had an opportunity of traveling on our new and elegant road.

As Mohomet, in despair of the mountain coming to him, condescended to make the mountain a visit, so our friend Beauregard—the hero of Sumter and Manassas—concluded that we were not at all anxious to enjoy that entertainment of "Southern powder and Southern steel" prepared for us, made up his mind to come and partake of our simple Northern cheer. And so, he came, bringing, as I am told, part of his army over our newly constructed road, without even going through with the formality of paying toll. He evidently intended remaining through the day, as he came before breakfast. Before he reached our camp, however, the morning meal was over, and we were preparing for inspection. But the sounding of the "long roll" through the camp told us that sterner work was at hand.

The regiment was formed, and, after remaining standing for a short time in the field where our camp was located, we marched in to a piece of timbered land to the south of us. Through this we advanced perhaps half a mile, to a sort of clearing, an occasional cannon ball passing over our heads, indicating the nature of the day's work before us. Reaching this clearing, we were ordered to lie down, and presently the firing commenced, and the contending parties were speedily engaged. The regiment that was advancing against us, was evidently an A, No. 1. One look at them was enough to convince a man that courage and discipline are virtues peculiar to neither North nor South. Without a waver the long line of glittering steel moved steadily forward, while, over all, the silken folds of the Confederate flag floated gracefully on the morning air. What regiment this was, I have not been able to ascertain positively. At first, I was told that it was the 8th Mississippi, but since then one of the prisoners has told me that it was the Crescent City Guard, from New Orleans. At all events, it was a superb one, and we speedily had the most convincing proof that it was good for something else besides to look at. At their left, and slightly in advance, was another regiment, of which I did not take so much notice. Both of these regiments did their best against us, while we were assisted by a section (2 pieces) of artillery.

After about half an hour of good work we were ordered back. At this point, judge that we must have suffered more than during any other part of the day. It was here that Henry Ady received his mortal wound. Wm. Ady was wounded here, and here Thomas Lewis received a shot through the shoulder. One of our men killed here, and more were wounded than during the balance of the day, although it could not have exceeded half an hour from the time we were ordered in until we were relieved. The order at length came to fall back, which was done in good order. And, by the way, must say that the regiment (I have not as yet learned who they were) that was in the fight before us, is not entitled to this praise. They came running back in the wildest disorder. One frightened fugitive in particular I noticed, who, as he came along and ran through our ranks, exclaimed: "Give them hell, boys. I gave them hell as long as I could." Whether he had really given them any of the sulfurous or not, I cannot say, but assuredly he had given them everything else he possessed, including his gun, cartridge-box, coat and hat, and was in a fair way to leave his unmentionables and undergarments, to be accounted for perhaps by the return so commonly made—"lost in action."

But to return. Our regiment was ordered to fall back, which we did in good style, and at the distance of perhaps a quarter of a mile our line of battle was reformed in a very creditable manner. Being so drawn up, a second time we advanced, halting at first on the brow of a slight elevation, tiring and by slow degrees advancing. This time most of the boys fired while standing. The line was also much more extended than at first—there being a regiment on our left and one, I believe, on our right. The enemy occupied about the same ground that we did at the time of the first attack by us—that is, they were firing from the same spot where we were lying about half an hour before. This time, I should say, we remained some three-quarters of an hour, and again fell back into the timber. Our ranks reformed and a third advance was made. This time we remained perhaps half an hour, when our cartridges having given out, it was directed that we go to the river for more ammunition.

This was for all practical purposes all the fighting done by our regiment during the day. How severe it was may be inferred from the fact that our regiment, numbering I think not more than six hundred men, lost about one hundred and eighty in killed and wounded. The Colonel was shot in the hand, the Lieut. Colonel in the ankle and the Major in the head. Both our regimental and company officers have shown themselves possessed of an abundance of pluck, and capacity for command.

There were some scenes positively ludicrous, although it was such a serious time. Some of our men were given to firing from some distance to the rear without thinking sufficiently who were in front, and in some instances wounded our own men, who were too far in advance of the regiment. One of these, with a view to protect himself from what he regarded the most dangerous fire, took position in front of a tree, having nothing between himself and the enemy, but a most excellent defense against the injudicious attacks of his own friends.

One little fellow in our company was wounded in the head at the time of our first advance, and while I poured water from my canteen on his wound, he gave me an account of the manner in which it was received, garnished with such an abundance of oaths that it would have made a sad inroad upon his pay, had the pecuniary penalties imposed by the third article of war upon "any non-commissioned officer or soldier who shall use any profane oath or execration," been strictly enforced. One of our greatest misfortunes was the want of suitable cartridges. The powder used in them was of such a poor quality that after firing the first few shots, our guns were so dirty that it was almost impossible to load them, the bullet being forced down with the greatest difficulty. Why such powder was used can only be explained on the supposition that poor powder costs less than good, and by using it somebody's friend, in the shape of an army contractor, made a "big thing" which might have been considerably reduced by use of the proper article.

Our march to the river was not a very regular affair, as each man got there as best he could and by his own route nevertheless we all, or nearly all of us who were unhurt, the first time learned was wounded. I came up on the bluffs when the regiment was forming and where several boxes of cartridges had been provided for the use of our regiment.

Again, we started back for the scene of action, but were ordered to take position in front of one of our batteries, which was situated about a half a mile back from the Landing and which at the time had not commenced firing. We remained there for a short time only, when we were directed to take another position half a mile in advance, where we remained nearly an hour. The enemy in the meantime were approaching us gradually but surely. The rattle of musketry during the whole day had been unceasing and at two or three o'clock it seemed to be increasing in fierceness and intensity. Our lines were assuredly giving way before the steady and vigorous attack of the rebel army, and while the masterly genius who directed their movements had infused his own spirit into their ranks, on our side there seemed to be something lacking.

The work assigned to us during the afternoon was exceedingly light. The order now came to fall back behind the battery. Other regiments had already passed us and taken their places there. The battery then opened. It was comprised of a good many pieces, among which my attention was principally attracted by a couple of monster guns, said to be one 84 and the other a 64-pounder. They belched forth their iron hail upon the advancing enemy, and should these fail, the word came from an old staff officer, our last and only resource was the bayonet. We were not forced to this dire alternative, however. The artillery proved to be very effective.

The day was rapidly drawing to a close. I can well remember when an urchin at school, with what satisfaction I used to see the lengthening shadows of evening come on, knowing school must soon close. I have viewed the same spectacle with the liveliest satisfaction when engaged in the eminently useful but somewhat laborious occupation of hoeing corn. Those who are accustomed to pay evening visits to young ladies assure me that the approach of evening is always hailed with pleasure. But never to the tired school boy never to the wearied laborer never to the ardent lover never even to that industrious poet, who was so much edified when "The curfew tolled the knell of parting day" not to Wellington, even, when at "red Waterloo he prayed that Blucher or night might soon come," was the close of day more welcome than it was to us when the golden chariot of the sun wheeled slowly down the West and passed out of sight.

Just before sunset, as our regiment—now fearfully reduced from killed, wounded and exhaustion, was standing in its place, a fresh regiment of Buell's command made its appearance and relieved us. Capt. Grant, of Co. A, who had been in command the after part of the day, directed us to a place of rendezvous, which was near an old house, in which but a few hours before a sutler was doing a thriving business. But commerce, you know, is proverbially timid, and trade does not flourish amid the rude clangor of arms. So, the sutler finding that it was unpleasant to transact business while cannon balls were flying through the roof of his establishment, had prudently abandoned it to its fate and taken care of himself. The judicial decision which pronounces pirates on the seas enemies of mankind and as such liable to capture by the ships of any nation, is paralleled by another decision—if not of the military courts, at least of most members of the profession, to the effect that sutlers are foes to the human or at least the soldier race, and their goods therefore lawful subjects of capture. I assure you the theory was acted upon promptly that night. A barrel of excellent crackers was the first to suffer, in the general scramble for the sutler's estate, of which I was so fortunate as to receive as many as my two hands would hold. With these and a chunk of cheese of most prodigious strength I made most excellent supper, after which a transient acquaintance of mine from Company I gave me a large paper of excellent smoking tobacco, which I feel confident he never obtained by any legitimate purchase. I sat down and filling my pipe, commenced musing over the affairs of the day, and you may well suppose my musings were not of a very agreeable character. The prospect was most decidedly blue— not the bright, cerulean tints of the summer sky, but a dark, despairing, deplorable blue.

That we were whipped was certain. That on the morrow we should all be taken prisoners was more than probable. Nothing but the appearance of Buell could save us from utter destruction. Fortunately, Buell was near at hand and all the night long we could hear the constant splashing of the steamboat wheels as regiment after regiment was brought over the stream. During the night, as if nature was disposed to add to the general gloom, a furious storm came on, which continued for several hours.

The gun-boats which had somehow obtained an idea of the position of the enemy kept up a pretty regular fire during the night. The roar of that firing was appalling, and the next day we learned that the effects of it had been destructive in the extreme. In the morning the enemy, acting on the maxim that "the early bird catches the worm," commenced operations bright and early. But during the whole day the tide of success rolled the other way. Not only had the force of Buell crossed the river, but Buell was with them, and it is no more than the truth to say that his personal presence was worth more than his whole army. Today we had generalship, yesterday chance seemed to rule the hour. The change was miraculous. Regiments the day before had gone into battle with no idea of what they were to do without support and with no provision for following up their success or recovering what they had lost. Today it was different, and for the first time we could perceive the difference between a scientific soldier, for such Buell assuredly is, and an imbecile character, which term describes somebody else.

Towards night, when it became evident that the enemy was in full retreat, we were near our old camp and concluded to stop there for the night, so turning the head of the regiment in that direction we came in about half an hour to the pleasant spot which some six and thirty hours before we had left under peculiar circumstances. Our home looked decidedly the worse for wear. In our principal avenue nearly in front of the captain's tent lay a dead horse. The tents were considerably torn by balls. In our tent was a six-pound ball which had torn quite a hole in the side of the edifice; two canister shot had also passed through it and left their marks behind them. When I saw these evidences of what had been the character of our visitors I could not help entertaining the inhospitable thought that I was glad I was not at home when they called. Our knapsacks had all been broken into. Our blankets were all taken. From my knapsack they had pilfered a pair of sky-blue pantaloons, which were my especial pride and joy, and in which I had been wont to array myself when preparing for any great occasion. The marauding vagabonds had carried off my Bible also, for what purpose I can't conceive, unless to have the ten commandments, and more especially the one which says, "thou shall not steal," hard by to refer to in case of need. I fared no worse than my neighbors, however. Each man lost something, and the Texan Rangers, who are generally supposed to have perpetrated the theft, are in consequence by no means popular.

 Since then we have remained here and are in daily expectation of moving forward or being attacked, but neither event has as yet happened. Perhaps I have been too jocose in giving a description of the fight as I saw it, but God knows I feel sad enough as often as I think of the dear friends who were stricken down to rise no more, and those who are lingering in pain and suffering.

I must now bring my letter to a close, not that I have told you the hundredth part of what I would like to, but I am kept somewhat busy now, and besides my conveniences are not of the best.

Cincinnati Times Account

*(This account from the correspondent of the **Cincinnati Times** gives a good overview of the battle. This version was excerpted in the **Port Tobacco Times and the Charles County Advertiser**, April 17, 1862.*

The Great Battle Near Corinth.

The correspondent of the *Cincinnati Times* gives the following account of the Pittsburg battle:

Our forces were stationed in the form of a semi-circle, the right resting on a point north of Crump's Landing, our center being in front of the main road to Corinth, and our left extending to the river, in the direction of Hamburg, four miles north of Pittsburg Landing.

At 2 o'clock on the morning of the 6th, 400 men from General Prentiss' division were attacked by the enemy, half a mile in advance of our lines. Our men fell back on the Twenty-Fifth Missouri, swiftly pursued by the enemy.

The advance of the rebels reached Colonel Peabody's brigade just as the long roll was sounded and the men were falling into line. The resistance was but short, and they retreated under a galling fire until they reached the second division.

At six o'clock the attack had become general along the entire front of our lines. The enemy, in large force, drove in the pickets of General Sherman's division, and fell on the Forty-eighth, Seventieth and Seventy Second Ohio regiments. These troops had never before been in action, and being so unexpectedly attacked, made as able a resistance as possible, but were, in common with the forces of Gen. Prentiss, compelled to seek support on the troops immediately in their rear.

At one o'clock the entire line of both sides was fully engaged. The roar of cannon and musketry was without intermission from the main center to a point extending half way down the left wing.

The rebels made a desperate charge on the Fourteenth Ohio Battery, and not being sufficiently sustained by infantry, it fell into their hands. Another severe fight occurred for the possession of the Fifth Ohio Battery, and three of its guns were taken by the enemy.

By eleven o'clock commanders of regiments had fallen, and in some cases not a single field officer remained; yet the fighting continued with an earnestness which showed that the contest on both sides was for death or victory. Foot by foot the ground was contested, and finding it impossible to drive back our center, the enemy slackened their fire and made a vigorous effort on our left wing, endeavoring to outflank and drive it to the river bank. This wing was under General Hurlburt, and was composed of the Fourteenth, Thirty-Second, Forty Fourth and Fifty-Seventh Indiana, Eighteenth and

Twenty-First Illinois. Fronting its line, however, were the Fifty-Fourth, Fifty-Seventh and Seventy-Seventh Ohio, and Fifth Ohio Cavalry, of Sherman's division.

For nearly two hours a sheet of fire blazed from both columns, the Rebels fighting with a valor that was only equaled by those contending with them. While the contest raged the hottest, the gunboat Tyler passed up the river to a point opposite the enemy, and poured in broadsides from her immense guns, greatly aiding in forcing the enemy back. Up to 3 o'clock the battle raged with a fury that defies description. The rebels had found their attempts to break our lines unavailing. They had striven to drive in our main column, and finding that impossible, had turned all their strength upon our left. Foiled in that quarter, they now made another attack on our center, and made every effort to rout our forces before the reinforcements which had been sent for should come up.

At five o'clock there was a short cessation in the firing of the enemy, their lines falling back for nearly half a mile. They suddenly wheeled, and again threw their entire force upon our left [unreadable sentence] but the gunboats Tyler and Lexington poured in their shot thick and fast with terrible effect.

In the meantime, General Lew Wallace, who had taken a circuitous route for Crump's Landing, appeared suddenly at the enemy's right wing. In the face of this combination of circumstances, the rebels felt that their enterprise that day was a failure, and as night was approaching, fell back until they reached an advantageous position somewhat in the rear of, yet occupying the main road to Corinth.

The gunboats continued to send their shell after them until they got out of range.

After a weary watch of several hours of intense anxiety, the advance regiment of General Buell's army appeared on the opposite bank of the river, and the work of crossing the river began. The Thirty-sixth Indiana and Sixty-Eighth Ohio being the first to cross, followed by the main portion of Nelson's and Bruce's divisions.

Cheer after cheer greeted their arrival, and they were immediately sent to the advance where they rested on their arms.

All night long steamers were engaged in ferrying Gen. Buell's forces across. When day light broke it was evident that the Rebels, too, had been strongly reinforced.

The Second Days Fight

The battle was opened by the rebels at 7 o'-clock, from the Corinth road, and in half an hour extended along the whole line.

At 9 o'clock the sound of artillery and musketry fully equaled that of the previous day. The enemy was met by the reinforcements and the still unwearied soldiers of yesterday with an energy they certainly could not have expected. It became evident that they were endeavoring with perseverance and determination to find some weak points by which to turn our forces. They left one point, but returned to it immediately, and they as suddenly, by some masterly stroke of generalship, directed a most vigorous attack upon some divisions where they fancied they would not be expected; but the fire of our lines was as steady as clock-work, and it soon became evident that the enemy considered the task he had undertaken a hopeless one.

Further reinforcements now began to arrive, and they, were posted on the right of the main center, under Wallace. Gens. Grant, Buell, Nelson, Sherman and Crittenden were everywhere present, directing the movements for a new stroke on the enemy. Suddenly, both wings of our army were turned upon the enemy, with the intention of driving them into an extensive ravine. At the same time a powerful battery was stationed in the open field and poured volley after volley of canister into the rebel ranks.

At 11 1/2 o'clock the roar of the battle shook the earth. The Union guns were fired with all the energy that the prospect of the enemy's defeat inspired, while the rebels' fire was not so vigorous, and they evinced a desire to withdraw.

They finally fell slowly back, keeping up a fire from their artillery and musketry along their whole column as they retreated. They moved in excellent order, battling at every advantageous point, and delivering their fire with considerable effect. But from all the divisions of our army they were closely pursued, a galling fire being kept upon their rear.

The enemy had now been driven beyond our former lines, and were in full retreat for Corinth, pursued by our cavalry.

Footnotes

[1] The Muscatine Weekly Journal. May 2, 1862.
[2] Grant, Ulysses S. Personal Memoirs of U. S. Grant. 1885 Vol. 1. P. 220.
[3] Sherman, William T. Memoirs of General William T. Sherman. 1884. Vol. 1. P. 279.
[4] Sherman, William T. Memoirs of General William T. Sherman. 1884. Vol. 1. P. 284.
[5] Evansville Daily Journal. March 1, 1862.
[6] Daily Ohio Statesman. February 19, 1862.
[7] Scott, Robert N. and Lazelle, Henry M. The War of the Rebellion: A Compilation of the Official Records of the Union and Confederate Armies. 1880-1901. Series 1. Vol. 9. Part 1. P. 270-271.
[8] The Chicago Daily Tribune. August 16, 1862.
[9] Scott, Colonel Robert N. The War of the Rebellion: A Compilation of the Official Records of the Union and Confederate Armies. Series 1. Vol. 10. 1884. P. 570.
[10] Robbins, Peggy. "Storm Over Fort Pulaski." America's Civil War. September 1990. P. 30.
[11] War of the Rebellion. 1880-1901. Series 1. Vol 14. P. 134.
[12] Daily Whig (Richmond). August 4, 1862.
[13] Grant, Ulysses S. Personal Memoirs of U. S. Grant. 1894. Vol. 1. P. 214.
[14] Scott, Colonel Robert N. The War of the Rebellion: A Compilation of the Official Records of the Union and Confederate Armies. Series 1. Vol. 10. 1884. P. 384-392.
[15] Smith, Timothy B. Rethinking Shiloh: Myth and Memory. 2013. P. 1.
[16] Scott, Colonel Robert N. The War of the Rebellion: A Compilation of the Official Records of the Union and Confederate Armies. Series 1. Vol. 10. Part 1. 1884. P. 463-470.
[17] Scott, Colonel Robert N. The War of the Rebellion: A Compilation of the Official Records of the Union and Confederate Armies. Series 1. Vol. 10. Part 1. 1884. P. 463-470.
[18] Scott, Colonel Robert N. The War of the Rebellion: A Compilation of the Official Records of the Union and Confederate Armies. Series 1. Vol. 10. Part 1. 1884. P. 463-470.
[19] Scott, Colonel Robert N. The War of the Rebellion: A Compilation of the Official Records of the Union and Confederate Armies. Series 1. Vol. 10.

Part 1. 1884. P. 463-470.

[20] Scott, Colonel Robert N. The War of the Rebellion: A Compilation of the Official Records of the Union and Confederate Armies. Series 1. Vol. 10. Part 1. 1884. P. 406.

[21] Scott, Colonel Robert N. The War of the Rebellion: A Compilation of the Official Records of the Union and Confederate Armies. Series 1. Vol. 10. Part 1. 1884. P. 407.

[22] Scott, Colonel Robert N. The War of the Rebellion: A Compilation of the Official Records of the Union and Confederate Armies. Series 1. Vol. 10. Part 1. 1884. P. 410.

[23] Scott, Colonel Robert N. The War of the Rebellion: A Compilation of the Official Records of the Union and Confederate Armies. Series 1. Vol. 10. Part 1. 1884. P. 410.

[24] Scott, Colonel Robert N. The War of the Rebellion: A Compilation of the Official Records of the Union and Confederate Armies. Series 1. Vol. 10. Part 1. 1884. P. 619.

[25] McClure, James Baird. Stories, Sketches and Speeches of General Grant: At Home and Abroad in Peace and War. 1879. P. 97-98.

[26] The New York Herald. December 19, 1861.

[27] Sherman, William T. Memoirs of General William T. Sherman. 1884. Vol. 1. P. 268.

[28] Sherman, William T. Memoirs of General William T. Sherman. 1884. Vol. 1. P. 275.

[29] Buell, Don Carlos. "Shiloh Reviewed." Battles and Leaders of the Civil War. Century Magazine. 1887. Vol. 1. P. 487.

[30] Buell, Don Carlos. "Shiloh Reviewed." Battles and Leaders of the Civil War. Century Magazine. 1887. Vol. 1. P. 487.

[31] Grant, Ulysses S. "The Battle of Shiloh." Battles and Leaders of the Civil War. Vol. 1. 1887. P. 468.

[32] Plummer, Mark A. Lincoln's Rail-splitter. Governor Richard Oglesby. P. 73.

[33] Scott, Colonel Robert N. The War of the Rebellion: A Compilation of the Official Records of the Union and Confederate Armies. Series 1. Vol. 10. 1884. P. 115.

[34] Scott, Colonel Robert N. The War of the Rebellion: A Compilation of the Official Records of the Union and Confederate Armies. Series 1. Vol. 10. 1884. P. 118.

[35] Scott, Colonel Robert N. The War of the Rebellion: A Compilation of the Official Records of the Union and Confederate Armies. Series 1. Vol. 10. 1884. P. 120.

[36] Scott, Colonel Robert N. The War of the Rebellion: A Compilation of the Official Records of the Union and Confederate Armies. Series 1. Vol. 10. 1884. P. 115.

[37] Scott, Colonel Robert N. The War of the Rebellion: A Compilation of the Official Records of the Union and Confederate Armies. Series 1. Vol. 10. 1884. P. 480.

[38] Scott, Colonel Robert N. The War of the Rebellion: A Compilation of the Official Records of the Union and Confederate Armies. Series 1. Vol. 10. 1884.

[39] Davenport Democrat. December 12, 1861.

[40] Originally printed in the Carrollton Press. Reprinted in the Juliet Signal. July 16, 1861.

[41] Scott, Colonel Robert N. The War of the Rebellion: A Compilation of the Official Records of the Union and Confederate Armies. Series 1. Vol. 10. 1884.

[42] Scott, Colonel Robert N. The War of the Rebellion: A Compilation of the Official Records of the Union and Confederate Armies. Series 1. Vol. 10. 1884. P. 567.

[43] Chicago Daily Tribune. August 14, 1862.

[44] Chicago Daily Tribune. August 14, 1862.

[45] Sherman, William Tecumseh and Sherman, John. The Sherman Letters: Correspondence Between General Sherman and Senator Sherman from 1837 to 1891. 1894. P. 115.

[46] Chicago Daily Tribune. August 14, 1862.

[47] Grant, Ulysses S. Personal Memoirs of Ulysses S. Grant. 1917. P. 280.

[48] Richmond Enquirer. June 17, 1864. "What the unfortunate butcher will do now we await to hear without the slightest feeling of anxiety."

[49] Dayton Daily Empire. September 30, 1864. The paper ran an article about a political rally against Abraham Lincoln, "the widow maker." The paper said, "One million and six hundred thousand men have been lost to their country by the imbecility of the flat boat clown and tyrant."

[50] Scott, Colonel Robert N. The War of the Rebellion: A Compilation of the Official Records of the Union and Confederate Armies. Series 1. Vol. 10. 1884. P. 278-279.

[51] Scott, Colonel Robert N. The War of the Rebellion: A Compilation of the Official Records of the Union and Confederate Armies. Series 1. Vol. 10. 1884. P. 281.

[52] Scott, Colonel Robert N. The War of the Rebellion: A Compilation of the Official Records of the Union and Confederate Armies. Series 1. Vol. 10. 1884. P. 292.

[53] Scott, Colonel Robert N. The War of the Rebellion: A Compilation of the Official Records of the Union and Confederate Armies. Series 1. Vol. 10. 1884. P. 478.

[54] Scott, Colonel Robert N. The War of the Rebellion: A Compilation of the Official Records of the Union and Confederate Armies. Series 1. Vol. 10. 1884. P. 479.

[55] Scott, Colonel Robert N. The War of the Rebellion: A Compilation of the Official Records of the Union and Confederate Armies. Series 1. Vol. 10. 1884. P. 279.

[56] Fleming, Robert H. "The Battle of Shiloh as a Boy Saw It." Sketches of War History, 1861-1865. Vol. VI. 1908.p. 136-137.

[57] Fleming, Robert H. "The Battle of Shiloh as a Boy Saw It." Sketches of War History, 1861-1865. Vol. VI. 1908.p. 136. Eagler was never arrested but says his commanding officer assured him Sherman issued the order.

[58] Reprinted in the Chicago Daily Tribune. August 14, 1862.

[59] Reprinted in the Chicago Daily Tribune. August 14, 1862.

[60] Grant, Ulysses S. Personal Memoirs of Ulysses S. Grant. 1917. P. 280-281.

[61] Andrew F. Davis Papers. University of Iowa Libraries. Special Collections. Box 1. http://digital.lib.uiowa.edu/cdm/compoundobject/collection/cwd/id/15087/rec/3

[62] Grant, Ulysses S. Personal Memoirs of Ulysses S. Grant. 1917. P. 280-283.

[63] Scott, Colonel Robert N. The War of the Rebellion: A Compilation of the Official Records of the Union and Confederate Armies. Series 1. Vol. 10. 1884. P. 571.

[64] Sherman, William Tecumseh and Sherman, John. The Sherman Letters: Correspondence Between General Sherman and Senator Sherman from 1837 to 1891. 1894. P. 117.

[65] The National Republican. April 18, 1862.

[66] Evening Star. April 10, 1862.

[67] Richmond Whig. April 11, 1862.

[68] Grant, Ulysses S. "The Battle of Shiloh." Battles and Leaders of the Civil War. Vol. 1. 1887. P. 483-484.

[69] Evening Star. April 10, 1862.

[70] Evening Star. April 16, 1862.

[71] Reprinted in The National Republican. April 18, 1862.

[72] Reprinted in The National Republican. April 18, 1862.

[73] Evening Star. April 11, 1862.

[74] Andrew F. Davis Papers. University of Iowa Libraries. Special Collections. Box 1. http://digital.lib.uiowa.edu/cdm/compoundobject/collection/cwd/id/15087/rec/3

[75] The Chicago Daily Tribune. August 16, 1862.

[76] Grant, Ulysses S. "The Battle of Shiloh." Battles and Leaders of the Civil War. Vol. 1. 1887. P. 468.

[77] Evening Star. April 11, 1862.

[78] Scott, Colonel Robert N. The War of the Rebellion: A Compilation of the Official Records of the Union and Confederate Armies. Series 1. Vol. 10. 1884. P. 575.

[79] The (Richmond, Virginia) Daily Dispatch. April 21, 1862.

[80] Scott, Colonel Robert N. The War of the Rebellion: A Compilation of the Official Records of the Union and Confederate Armies. Series 1. Vol. 10. 1884. P. 570.

[81] Evening Star. April 18, 1862.

[82] Evening Star. April 18, 1862.

[83] Evening Star. April 16, 1862.

[84] Buell, Don Carlos. "Shiloh Reviewed." Battles and Leaders of the Civil War. Vol. 1. 1887. P. 487.

[85] Buell, Don Carlos. "Shiloh Reviewed." Battles and Leaders of the Civil War. Vol. 1. 1887. P. 487-536.

[86] Sherman, William Tecumseh and Sherman, John. The Sherman Letters: Correspondence Between General Sherman and Senator Sherman from 1837 to 1891. 1894. P. 114.

[87] Grant was very careful to call these backward movements, not retreats. It made the backward movements sound as if they were part of the plan.

[88] Sherman, William Tecumseh and Sherman, John. The Sherman Letters: Correspondence Between General Sherman and Senator Sherman from 1837 to 1891. 1894. P. 137.

[89] Grant, Ulysses S. "The Battle of Shiloh." Battles and Leaders of the Civil War. 1887. Vol. 1. P. 465.

[90] Daily Ohio Statesman. March 3, 1867.

[91] Muscatine Weekly Journal. May 2, 1862.

[92] The New York Herald. April 11, 1862.

[93] The Chicago Daily Tribune. April 16, 1862.

[94] The Chicago Daily Tribune. April 16, 1862.

[95] The National Republican. April 15, 1862.

[96] Scott, Colonel Robert N. The War of the Rebellion: A Compilation of the Official Records of the Union and Confederate Armies. Series 1. Vol. 10.

1884. P. 568.

Made in the USA
Middletown, DE
20 April 2022